Sarah-Jane Pill

Understanding the Intercultural Differences between Germans and French in the Working Environment

An Empirical Analysis through Application of the Cultural Assimilator

Bachelorarbeit
Fachhochschule Deggendorf
Studiengang International Management (B.A.)
Abgabe August 2005

Diplomica GmbH
Hermannstal 119k
22119 Hamburg

Fon: 040 / 655 99 20
Fax: 040 / 655 99 222

agentur@diplom.de
www.diplom.de

ID 9225
Pill, Sarah-Jane:
Understanding the Intercultural Differences between Germans and French in the Working
Environment - An Empirical Analysis through Application of the Cultural Assimilator
Hamburg: Diplomica GmbH, 2006
Zugl.: Fachhochschule Deggendorf, Bachelorarbeit, 2005

Dieses Werk ist urheberrechtlich geschützt. Die dadurch begründeten Rechte, insbesondere die der Übersetzung, des Nachdrucks, des Vortrags, der Entnahme von Abbildungen und Tabellen, der Funksendung, der Mikroverfilmung oder der Vervielfältigung auf anderen Wegen und der Speicherung in Datenverarbeitungsanlagen, bleiben, auch bei nur auszugsweiser Verwertung, vorbehalten. Eine Vervielfältigung dieses Werkes oder von Teilen dieses Werkes ist auch im Einzelfall nur in den Grenzen der gesetzlichen Bestimmungen des Urheberrechtsgesetzes der Bundesrepublik Deutschland in der jeweils geltenden Fassung zulässig. Sie ist grundsätzlich vergütungspflichtig. Zuwiderhandlungen unterliegen den Strafbestimmungen des Urheberrechtes.

Die Wiedergabe von Gebrauchsnamen, Handelsnamen, Warenbezeichnungen usw. in diesem Werk berechtigt auch ohne besondere Kennzeichnung nicht zu der Annahme, dass solche Namen im Sinne der Warenzeichen- und Markenschutz-Gesetzgebung als frei zu betrachten wären und daher von jedermann benutzt werden dürften.

Die Informationen in diesem Werk wurden mit Sorgfalt erarbeitet. Dennoch können Fehler nicht vollständig ausgeschlossen werden, und die Diplomarbeiten Agentur, die Autoren oder Übersetzer übernehmen keine juristische Verantwortung oder irgendeine Haftung für evtl. verbliebene fehlerhafte Angaben und deren Folgen.

Diplomica GmbH
http://www.diplom.de, Hamburg 2006
Printed in Germany

Table of contents

Preface 7

1 Introduction of the Topic 8

    1.1 Problem 9

    1.2 Objective 9

    1.3 Scope and Limitations 10

    1.4 Outline 10

2 Determining Factors of Intercultural Interaction 11

    2.1 Culture 11

        2.1.1 What is Culture? 11

        2.1.2 Influence of National Culture on Corporate Culture 14

    2.2 Communication 15

        2.2.1 Cross-Cultural Communication 15

        2.2.2 Communication Barriers 17

    2.3 Intercultural Competence 18

        2.3.1 Acquiring Intercultural Competence in Today's Business World 18

        2.3.2 The Danger of Stereotyping 20

3 Key Models of Cultural Dimensions 22

    3.1 Hofstede and his Dimensions of Culture 22

        3.1.1 Power Distance 23

        3.1.2 Individualism vs. Collectivism 24

        3.1.3 Femininity vs. Masculinity 24

        3.1.4 Uncertainty Avoidance 25

    3.2 Hall's Dimensions of Culture 26

        3.2.1 High Context vs. Low Context 26

        3.2.2 Space 27

        3.2.3 Time 28

	3.3 Comparison of the two Models 28
	3.3.1 Critical Observation of Hofstede's Dimensions 29
	3.3.2 Critical Observation of Hall's Framework 29

4 Germany and France 31

4.1 Germany 31

    4.1.1 Historical Background 32

    4.1.2 Culture and Society 33

    4.1.3 Education System 34

    4.1.4 Economy 35

4.2 France 36

    4.2.1 Historical Background 37

    4.2.2 Culture and Society 38

    4.2.3 Education System 39

    4.2.4 Economy 40

5 The Approach of Germany and France in Everyday Life and Business 41

5.1 Development of the Relationship between Germany and France 41

    5.1.1 Historical Development of the Bilateral Relations 42

    5.1.2 Political Relations 45

    5.1.3 Economic Relations 46

    5.1.4 Cultural Relations 47

    5.1.5 Cooperation in the Field of Education 48

5.2 Business Culture between French and German Companies 49

    5.2.1 Management Style 49

        5.2.1.1 The Role of the Boss 50

        5.2.1.2 Decision-making Style 51

        5.2.1.3 Power vs. Money 52

    5.2.2 Differing Attitudes to Work 53
        5.2.2.1 Task-Orientation vs. People-Orientation 54
        5.2.2.2 Functionality vs. Perfection 55
        5.2.2.3 Innovation vs. Conservatism 56
        5.2.2.4 Motivation – The Key for a Successful Cooperation 57
6 Empirical Review of the Culture Clash between French and Germans 59
    6.1 The Concept of Cultural Assimilator 59
        6.1.1 Research Method 60
            6.1.1.1 Description of Sample 60
            6.1.1.2 Research Design 60
            6.1.1.3 Method of Collecting Information 61
            6.1.1.4 Limitations 62
    6.2 Critical Incidents 63
        6.2.1 Student-Teacher Relationship 63
            6.2.1.1 Possible Solutions 63
            6.2.1.2 Explanation 64
        6.2.2 An Unanswered Email 66
            6.2.2.1 Possible Solutions 66
            6.2.2.2 Explanation 66
        6.2.3 Business Negotiation 67
            6.2.3.1 Possible Solutions 68
            6.2.3.2 Explanation 68
        6.2.4 Time Management 69
            6.2.4.1 Possible Solutions 70
            6.2.4.2 Explanation 70
        6.2.5 An Act of Friendship 71
            6.2.5.1 Possible Solutions 71
            6.2.5.2 Explanation 72

| 6.2.6 A Chaotic Meeting..73

              6.2.6.1 Possible Solutions...73

              6.2.6.2 Explanation 74

       6.3 Suggestions for a Better Cooperation with French People......................................75

7   Conclusion...76

Bibliography 77

Appendix A: Questionnaire Interviewees 83

Table of Figures

Fig. 1: Three levels of human mental programming 13

Fig. 2: What Germans mean when they say 16

Fig. 3: Geert Hofstede 22

Fig. 4: Edward T. Hall 26

Fig. 5: 40th Anniversary - Elysée Treaty 41

Fig. 6: Voisins et Enemies 42

Fig. 7: Reconciliation between Adenauer and the Gaulle 44

Fig. 8: The academic mobility between Germany and France 48

Fig. 9: Need a strong management. "This feels good!" 51

Fig. 10: Meeting between Germans and French 54

Preface

The following analysis focuses on the examination of the French and German culture and its significance to the working environment. Although being neighbouring countries, the intercultural understanding between French and Germans is not always evident, but it is becoming more and more important in the era of a growing Europe.

During a six-month stay in the South of France, I worked as a volunteer in a Youth Information Centre. Although working in a public organization may not be comparable with being employed in a company, I was able to get an insight into French business life. Another stay in the South East of France enabled me to get to know university life for a period of five months. My friendships with the local people revealed various differences between the German and the French culture. Moreover, during a six-month internship in the international Marketing department of OSRAM GmbH in Germany, I experienced what difficulties may arise as a result of intercultural misunderstandings.

Even though the quantity of literature available on French and German culture has expanded over several years, I was astonished to find out how little people knew about their neighbouring country and its culture. Even in international business, cultural differences are neglected, and the national culture is often regarded as superior.

I therefore decided to analyse the reasons for misunderstandings between French and Germans in order to contribute to a better understanding of the culture of our French neighbours.

Finally, I would like to thank all people who gave me great support during the compilation phase of my thesis. Special thanks go to the *Deutsch Französisches Institut*, who supported my scientific research in their library. Thanks also to my various French and German interview partners from Osram GmbH, Bollhoff-Otalu S.A., MAN, as well as to many students who were eager to tell me about their internship experiences. I want to thank all my friends who supported my work by asking questions, expressing criticism and making helpful suggestions. Last but not least, I am very grateful for the support and understanding of my boyfriend Philipp, my parents and Kylie who showed great patience in proofreading.

1 Introduction of the Topic

"In an ideal world, the policemen would be English, the car mechanics German, the cooks would be French, the bankers Swiss, and the lovers Italian. But in the real world, we must not forget that there are also policemen that are German, car mechanics that are French, cooks that are English, bankers that are Italian and lovers that are Swiss." (www.analytictech.com)

Internationalisation and globalisation have an enormous affect on every day life. The number and intensity of contacts - in business life, school, apprenticeship, advanced training or in private life - between people from different cultures is ever-increasing.

Due to a growing number of international companies and mergers, working together with foreign colleagues has become a usual occurrence for many people. It is therefore a central topic of the 21st century to cope with cultural diversity and develop intercultural competence.

Looking back at history, interaction between cultures is nothing new. Interstate contacts and intercultural processes have always been the result of political, military, economic and religious actions. In the majority of cases, the enlargement and stabilisation of the power structure were the fundamental causes for these processes.

Due to an expanding transportation system and technological progress, globalisation has entered a new dimension. Nowadays, information can be passed on across the globe easily and inexpensively; exchanges between schools, universities or businesses have become a stable feature; travelling around the world is no longer the privilege of the rich.

Accordingly, there are several areas of life affected by cross-cultural interactions; a very complex one is the working environment, which is the subject of this thesis.

1.1 Problem

Understanding the dynamics of international business encounters requires a fundamental shift from comparative studies of cultural differences to the study of intercultural interactions. The decisive issue in international management is not the existence of differences, but the way behavioural differences are perceived, interpreted, and managed by members of different national cultures.

This research will clarify the intercultural aspects of business relations between *French* and *Germans*. Why is *this* relationship of such great interest?

As the European Union grows, the idea of a European identity is spread among its member countries. Although these countries have a relatively close geographical position towards each other, there are still cultural differences (Barmeyer, 1996). In particular, the relationship between Germany and France shows that these differences persist and have even increased since the reunification of Germany in 1990 (Chevènement, 1996). Despite the establishment of numerous programs and institutions, with the aim of improving intercultural relations between these two countries, stereotypes and prejudices still exist on both sides of the Rhine. According to several publications and studies, everyday life as well as business life is equally affected by the inharmoniousness caused by these cultural differences (Breuer & de Bartha, 2002). Frequently, business negotiations and even mergers between German and French companies fail due to intercultural misunderstandings and the problems involved.

1.2 Objective

The aim of this thesis is to illustrate intercultural conflict potential between French and Germans in business life and to establish a better understanding of the French culture.

Behaviour patterns are an expression of various influences over the centuries. In order to acquire intercultural competence of a country, it is important to know about its applied geography and the consistencies in its economy, history and the cultural dimensions. Therefore, all of the relevant available data is used to describe specific characteristics, attitudes as well as typical behavioural patterns of Germans and French, which are often contradictory. How this can lead to problems and misunderstandings in business life, and how intercultural barriers can be overcome, will be shown in an empirical analysis based on interviews with French and Germans. The results will be presented, analysed, and explained using the Cultural Assimilator method, which is based on information given in the theoretical part.

1.3 Scope and Limitations

The plenitude of researches about German-French relations can hardly be ignored. Most works deal with the bilateral development concerning history, politics, and economy. Among these numerous books, there are only a few addressing the intercultural relations between France and Germany. Therefore, this thesis focuses on the intercultural understanding between both countries.

1.4 Outline

The first part consists of a theoretical review of literature that is designed to gather important information of the numerous academic publications on culture. Its intention is to enable the reader to develop a thorough understanding of the cultural concept. It includes the definition of culture and the illustration of how company culture is influenced by national culture. Furthermore, the term intercultural competence and how it is acquired is explained. After specifying the dangers of stereotyping, the cultural dimensions of two famous authors in this field, Hofstede and Hall, are presented. This part ends with a critical evaluation of the two concepts. The following chapters contain a general approach towards France and Germany including history, culture and society, educational system and economy. Subsequently, an overview of the relationship between the two countries will be delivered. The theoretical part, which aims at preparing the reader for the practical part of the thesis, ends with a detailed comparison about the different attitudes of French and Germans concerning business life.

The second, empirical part of the thesis contains critical situations between French and Germans, which have been collected using the qualitative research method. After a description of the research method, which includes a characterisation of the sample, the concept of the Cultural Assimilator is explained in detail. By applying this concept, the reader needs to resort to theoretical information, given in the first part, which shall increase his awareness of intercultural problems occurring in ordinary business life.

2 Determining Factors of Intercultural Interaction

Experience abroad has become indispensable for management positions. Therefore, more and more young people leave their home countries for a certain period of time in order to acquire international experience. A lot of intercultural knowledge is acquired by travelling, but even if someone has not yet been abroad, he/she will certainly know various facts about other countries and their culture. Unfortunately this knowledge is often based on word of mouth and as the topic of interculturality seems relatively easy to understand, a lot of people are certain they have become experts in intercultural relations after having spent just two weeks abroad. Although, experience abroad is the basis of acquiring knowledge about the culture of a country, one should first become familiar with the terms used in the context of intercultural interactions. Even famous authors writing about this subject often differ considerably on their definition of culture. Therefore, the following part focuses on exploring more deeply on the real meaning of culture, communication and intercultural competence.

2.1 Culture

The word culture is derived from the Latin root *colere* meaning "to inhabit", "to cultivate", or "to honour". Originated during the 18th and 19th century in Europe, it was used to differentiate more civilised from less civilized cultures. Since then, several definitions of the word *culture* have been developed (Wikipedia, 05/2005).

The next part explains the meaning of culture, cultural standards, as well as the impact of culture on business life.

2.1.1 What is Culture?

In 1998, Scarborough describes culture as "[...] the set of values, attitudes, and beliefs shared by [...] a group, which sets the standards of behaviour required for continued acceptance and successful participation in that group" (Scarborough, 1998, p. 1). According to a declaration on cultural diversity issued by the agency of the United Nations, UNESCO (2002), "[...] culture should be regarded as the set of distinctive spiritual, material, intellectual and emotional features of society or a social group, and that it encompasses, in addition to art and literature, lifestyles, ways of living together, value systems, traditions and beliefs." Based on these two definitions, common ways of perception, thinking, behaviour patterns and values are inherent in every culture. These values and norms, which are accepted and commonly used in a society, facilitate the well-ordered coexistence of mankind. The central aspects of this orientation system are known as 'cultural standards' – ranging from general values to binding rules. The behaviour of people at home or abroad is judged according to these cultural standards, which define the range of tolerance. Different cultures can have similar cultural standards, but they may have developed in a different way so that they might only be noticed in certain situations or are perceived less important (Thomas, 1999).

According to what has been said until now, it is important to reiterate that culture should not be confused with nationality as there are groups who share the same cultural values across geographical boundaries (Gibson, 1998).

For the most part, these shared values and behaviour patterns are exercised unconsciously or as Hofstede states in a different way "culture is the collective programming of the mind […]" (Hofstede, 1974, p. 5). This collective programming of mindset and behaviour is "passed on, learned by newcomers from more experienced predecessors" (Scarborough, 1998, p. 1), in other words, values, rituals, perceptions, preferences and attitudes are transmitted from generation to generation, they are not inherited or genetic (Hofstede, 1997).

From infancy, children are told by their parents how to behave politely in social situations, they are taught good table manners and that certain rules should be obeyed. Besides the family, teacher, friends, which coin the child's behaviour, other key figures like charismatic leaders, religion, political power, physical surroundings and economy can shape culture and therefore our core beliefs (Scarborough, 1998; Lewis, 1996): the Islam, for instance, highly influences the core values of its adherents; people living in communist countries are affected by the constant fight for democracy; Eskimos adjust their living style to the prevailing harsh climate. Depending on the success of an economy, inhabitants of the developing world have formed other family values than those living in developed countries.

In his model of mental programming (see Fig. 1, illustrated on the next page), Hofstede (1997) clarifies the difference between *human nature,* which expresses the congenital skills of every human being like the ability to fear, to communicate, to associate, and *culture* which originates from one's social environment. Consequently, someone's personality is influenced by culture combined with unique personal experiences.

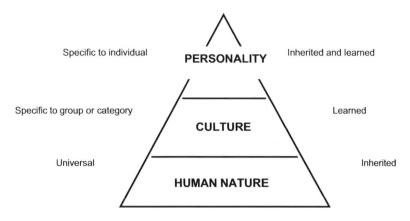

Fig. 1: Three levels of uniqueness in human mental programming

So far, the definition of the word *culture*, which represents shared values of a given group, has been defined in detail. Furthermore, it was analysed how human values develop and in which way they influence the behaviour of individuals. Based on this knowledge, the next chapter provides answers to the question "what will happen if a culture correlates with another one?" "When people of one culture compare themselves to another, they tend to see their own culture as normal and superior and the other as aberrational and inferior" (Scarborough, 1998, p. 14). People tend to regard other cultures as extrinsic because they are different from their own (Lewis, 1996).

In which way does a culture alter if confronted with another culture? How do humans react to foreign values and behaviour patterns? Will they adapt their attitude? Are employees less efficient when working in a multinational environment? And, after all, what impact does national culture have on corporate culture? The following paragraphs will provide further details on these questions.

2.1.2 Influence of National Culture on Corporate Culture

National culture[1] exerts great influence on global behaviour patterns as well as on company's overall corporate culture; or as Breuer and de Bartha (2002) would put it "die Landeskultur legt sich wie ein Ring um die Unternehmenskultur"[2] (p. 69).

Management e.g. is based on creative processes, which are formed intensely by culture and national originalities (Breuer & de Bartha, 2002). As a result of universally accepted values shared by country's inhabitants, employees either prefer a directive or participating management style (Hofstede, 1997).

National culture also affects important everyday business practices like: communication, decision-making processes, employer-employee relationship, motivation, and timing. More details concerning these issues will be provided later in this thesis.

Although there have been many attempts to impose a certain corporate culture on employees, there is no chance for principles, disposed by a company to advance efficiency, unless they comply with the national culture (Pateau, 1999). If there is a high conformity between national culture and business values, the implementation will be easier and faster. If these values collide, however, national culture will hinder the intrusion of the principles and will lead to a delay of new management models (Hahn, 1999). Hence, corporate culture does not deactivate national culture.

According to the given information, corporate culture emerges from a national culture model. Therefore, it is hardly impossible to carry over a corporate culture, which is efficient in one country, on another culture. As a consequence, it is inevitable not to deal with the cultural dimensions of a country when implementing business culture. Pateau, 1999

---

[1] The word *national culture*, as used in this chapter, refers to the culture of one country. It might seem controversial to speak of *national culture* although it was stated before that there might be similar cultural traits beyond the national frontiers. Unfortunately it is inevitable to generalise when knowledge of the culture of a specific country is imparted, as it is the purpose of this thesis (Breuer & de Bartha, 2002).

[2] *Suggested translation by the author:* "the national culture encircles the corporate culture."

2.2 Communication

"Communication is the process of exchanging information usually via a common system of symbols" (Dance, 1970, p. 201). People communicate in order to share information, thoughts, knowledge and experiences. Typical ways of communication include sign language, gestures, writing or speaking. A lot of signs and gestures occur without knowledge. Thus, the SEL Foundation in Stuttgart, Germany, found out that two people exchange, analyse and process over 400,000 signals within a 30-minutes conversation (Breuer & de Bartha, 2002). Since the communication style is influenced by one's culture, the following part is aimed at investigating how people from different cultural backgrounds try to communicate with one another and the difficulties that may arise.

2.2.1 Cross-Cultural Communication

Cultural growth in the 21st century has heightened the emphasis on communication in an intercultural setting. As the globalisation proceeds and the world becomes more and more interconnected by means of technological advances, the need for effective cross-cultural communication among different cultures is of increasing importance (Gibson, 1998).

The term *Cross-Cultural Communication*, also known as *Intercultural Communication*, dates back to 1959, which was according to Hart (1997), the same year in which Hall, a famous author in this field, published his work „The silent language". Pusch and Hoopes (1979) stated that Hall's work "gave us the first comprehensive analysis of the relationship between communication and culture" (p. 10). Cross-Cultural Communication can be defined as the area of study that attempts to understand the effects of culture on communication (Hart, 1997).

Besides language, following behavioural concepts play an important role in intercultural communication: kinesics (body movements), proxemics (space organisation), oculesics (eye movement), haptics (touching behaviour) as well as paralinguistic concepts, such as accents, intonation, speed of talking and so on (Dahl, 2004).

In order to illustrate the difficulties, which may occur between two different cultures during a conversation, Dahl (2004) refers to the eye contact, which is a very important means of communication in Western countries, whereas in Asian countries constant eye contact is unacceptable. It becomes obvious that this difference may lead to misunderstandings between people of different cultures.

The act of handshaking is another example to show how a conversation can be influenced by culture from the beginning. If we refer to the French custom of handshaking, it can be noticed that the handshake of the French is relatively light and easy whereas Germans shake hands in a tighter way. For Germans weak handshaking is considered as discourteous behaviour. In France, however, a tight handshake may be regarded as uncivilised or even harassing (Breuer & de Bartha, 2002).

Fig. 2: What Germans mean when they say…

The above picture illustrates that people do not always expect the same answer when asking a question. Here the American just wants to be friendly by asking the German "how are you?" expecting only a short answer. Above all, he does not want to hear something negative about the person's present state of affairs. Unlike the American, the German expresses gratitude for the sympathy shown and consequently reports in detail how he really feels.

Being aware of the fact that culture influences communication, it is also important to keep in mind that "the essence of effective cross cultural communication has more to do with releasing the right response than with sending the "right" message" (Hall, 1990, p. 4) or according to Breuer and de Bartha (2002): the basis of communication is a good relationship - frankness and trust.

Nevertheless, there are fundamental communication barriers, which will be further clarified in the next section.

2.2.2 Communication Barriers

A retired German businessman, who had worked in Paris for several years, explained during an interview conducted for this thesis "Natürlich konnte ich Französisch sprechen, aber wenn es um wichtige Dinge ging, war immer ein Dolmetscher vor Ort. Zum Beispiel bei Vertragsunterzeichnungen - am Schluß hätte ich noch den Franzosen meine Firma verkauft und es nicht einmal gemerkt!"[3] This example shows clearly that language is an important and often indispensable means of communication. One might expect that nowadays speaking the English language would be sufficient to communicate with people from foreign countries. This is probably true for some countries, but due to reasons explained later, in France for instance, one is almost lost without knowing at least a few words of French. "Auf französischer wie auf deutscher Seite ist man sich […] einig darüber, daß Kompetenzen in der jeweils anderen Sprache eine wesentliche Voraussetzung für die interkulturelle Verständigung schlechthin darstellen"[4] (Zimmermann, 1995, p. 153).

In addition, differences in body language, which were described earlier (see 2.1.1), as well as one's mental attitude, may lead to intercultural misunderstandings. Varieties in motivation and working habits, or fear of the other culture, may also cause serious problems and result in project failure (Breuer & de Bartha, 2002).

Another prominent barrier of intercultural communication is the notion of *Self-fulfilling-prophecy*. This term describes a situation, which will be positive or negative depending on one's prior perception. The following example of school life illustrates this effect: The performance of a student may be influenced in a positive or negative way, merely by the teacher's expectations; they can be so strong that the student will act accordingly. The same is true for numerous other examples, e.g. an interaction between a German and a French businessman: When a French is late for a meeting; the German will find the stereotype of the unpunctual French affirmed and reacts cool on the arrival of his counterpart. The French businessman, however, will judge the German's behaviour as unfriendly and cold. Breuer & de Bartha, 2002; Pateau, 1999

---

[3] *Suggested translation by the author:* "Of course I was able to speak French, but for matters of great importance we always used the service of an interpreter. E. g. when agreements had to be signed – in the end, I might have ended up selling my company to the French without even noticing it."

[4] *Suggested translation by the author:* "French as well as German experts agree that foreign language skills are an absolute must for intercultural understanding."

In order to overcome these existing difficulties, *Intercultural Competence* plays an important role in international business. The next chapter will explain this term as well as the problems involved in acquiring intercultural knowledge.

2.3 Intercultural Competence

As stated on the website of the Centre of Intercultural Competence (02/2005) "Intercultural competence is the ability for successful communication with people of other cultures."

Tensions occur frequently in everyday life, for example, between different individuals of the same culture. The competence required to solve interpersonal problems is called *social competence* which is the basis of intercultural competence, (Breuer & de Bartha, 2002), or, as the author Stefan Zweig puts it, "Wer einmal den Menschen in sich begriffen hat, der begreift alle Menschen"[5] (Breuer & de Bartha 2002, p. 71). In addition to social competence, the knowledge of cultural dimensions, as well as communication skills constitutes an important part of intercultural competence (Barmeyer, 1999).

Having made these brief introductory remarks about the term of intercultural competence, the key to intercultural competence and how it can be improved will be investigated in the first part of the next chapter. The second part will cover the direct link between intercultural competence and the risk of lumping together all individuals of one culture regarding their behaviour patterns.

2.3.1 Acquiring Intercultural Competence in Today's Business World

Intercultural conflicts, the failure of projects and even the collapse of mergers between companies of different cultures resulting in immense costs (Pateau, 1999), were the reason for many board members to rethink their strategy. In order to train expatriates for their future job in a new environment, many companies nowadays offer, in addition to language courses, intercultural seminars to convey intercultural awareness to their employees (and sometimes also to their spouses). There are a large number of companies specialised in intercultural training. These seminars usually last between one and several days and are often held by people who have

---

[5] *Suggested translation by the author:* "Someone who has understood the human as such will be able to understand all humans."

lived in the relevant country. Basic knowledge of history, culture, eating habits and specialties are taught by using various methods (presentations, role plays, etc.).

However, these intercultural training lessons are limited to particular countries. The person responsible for Osram's expatriates stated that in her company intercultural seminars are only offered to expatriates who are sent to Asian countries; European countries are often neglected due to the geographical closeness. This attitude can be described as "kulturelle Blindheit"[6] (cited in Barmeyer, 1999, p. 373), which leads to an underestimation of the influence of culture. Barmeyer, 1999

Although, cultural differences for European countries are being neglected, it can be said, that the number of intercultural seminars offered has considerably increased. While this development is a positive one, the following questions should be analyzed more closely: Are one or two days of intercultural training sufficient for getting to know a new culture well and thus acquiring intercultural competence? Are there any cultures, which are so similar to ours that it is not necessary to have an extensive training?

Interestingly, 2 out of 21 French and German interview partners conducted for this thesis, considered *an intercultural preparation for working together with French/Germans* (see appendix A: questionnaire interviewees) as unnecessary. Later in the interview, every one of them named at least one misunderstanding and several difficulties in the interaction with the other culture - an intercultural seminar might have prevented some of these problems. This attitude is demonstrated by the experience of two consultants for intercultural relations: Breuer and de Bartha (2002). In their book "Deutsch-französische Geschäftsbeziehungen erfolgreich managen", they explain that they are not consulted until a company is in *serious* trouble due to intercultural misunderstandings, or to put it shortly, if it is already too late.

One reason for this might be that today's managers focus on working efficiently and therefore believe a language course, a one day seminar or sometimes even a book dealing with the relevant subject, is sufficient to learn how to interact professionally with the other culture. This success-oriented thinking also explains why intercultural training seminars for expatriates sent to European countries are often viewed as unnecessary.

---

[6] *Suggested translation by the author:* "cultural blindness"

Language courses, intercultural training seminars, books, and conversations with experienced colleagues are means of helping people to acquire intercultural awareness or intercultural competence. This intercultural *knowledge* alone, however, is insufficient, as the following example will illustrate.

People are often aware of cultural differences, e.g. it is widely known that people from Southern countries are not very punctual. What happens if a French businessman is late at a meeting scheduled with his German colleague? If the German is aware of the different time perception of the French, he probably will not mention it, although he considers being late as inefficient. Nevertheless, the meeting will be influenced by stress and silent accusation of the German, which will surely be noticed by his French partner (Breuer & de Bartha, 2002).

Furthermore, technical knowledge will no longer suffice in order to be successful in intercultural business. Intercultural sensibility, understanding, the willingness to adjust to cultural rules, norms and customs of the other country are highly demanded qualifications and can contribute to a competitive advantage over a business rival. A basic requirement is to have a thorough knowledge of other cultures, but also of one's own culture (Thomas, Kinast & Schroll-Machl, 2003). Moreover, it is important to accept that the behaviour of the people of other cultures is not better or worse, but simply different (Hecht-El Minshawi, 2003). Therefore, it is essential to understand why other cultures act in a certain way. Moreover, the behaviour of other cultures should not be measured on one's own cultural standards.

Intercultural competence also means being aware of generalisations and prejudices. It is obvious that in a research about cultures, there is a certain danger of lumping together people belonging to the same culture, which will be dealt with in the following chapter.

2.3.2 The Danger of Stereotyping

In describing a culture, generalisations are being made, i.e. simplified mental pictures of an individual or a group of people sharing certain characteristic qualities are portrayed.

According to Scarborough (1998) "we confront the issue of stereotyping". This term is often used in a negative sense, nevertheless it is correct to characterize a group of people as being different from another one, not just because of their physical appearance. Cultural anthropologists use the term *core values* to define the values that describe a group most accurately.

However, it has to be kept in mind that, although people are often referred to as 'typically German' or 'typically American', there is no reason for assuming that an individual possesses all values of that person's culture since everyone has a unique personality (Scarborough, 1998). Considering the French and the Germans, for instance, there are French people who can rather be assigned to German core values depending on their business / private life or vice versa (Breuer & de Bartha, 2002).

The danger lies in a one-sided conception, i.e. people usually have a pre-established picture of a foreign individual in mind, even if they have never been in contact with somebody of that culture. These socially inherited theories, resulting from the judgment of a case before it has been understood, can be classified as prejudgment, prejudice or discrimination (Schäfer & Jung, 1994). Usually, these prejudices are not formed by first-hand experience, but passed on through tradition, transmission and mediation. They are also extremely resistant to experiences which are not in accordance with the preconceived image, as Berting (1995) explains "we tend to ignore the social conditions of our social and cultural experiences and we tend to declare, finally, that those phenomena which do not fit our idea or image of the outside world are 'not important' when we are forced to perceive them." (p. 13).

In research papers on cultural differences, nationality is often used as a criterion to classify cultures. The same approach will be applied in this analysis; generalisations are therefore inevitable. This is due to the fact that data on nations, for example population statistics, can be obtained much easier than on homogeneous societies. Besides, the collection of data on a national level provides a basis for encouraging harmonisation among nations. Today, over 200 nations live together very closely and interact with each other. In order to unite people, it is therefore essential to focus on cultural factors and learn about them (Hofstede, 1991).

Reading the following chapters, it is very important to keep in mind that not every person has the same traits whenever referring to French or Germans. It is not the purpose of this thesis to convey the absolute truth, but to identify general behavioural tendencies, which frequently cause misunderstandings and conflicts.

3 Key Models of Cultural Dimensions

Cultural dimensions are mostly psychological dimensions, or value constructs, which have been developed in order to identify the differences and similarities of local, regional and international cultures. Comparing the experiences and difficulties people come across when corresponding with foreign individuals, numerous similarities can be noticed. Although cultural dimensions are generalisations, they provide an informative basis when comparing cultures systematically. Furthermore, they might be very helpful in understanding why people from other cultures act differently (Hecht-El Minshawi, 2003).

The following chapter provides an outline of the models of cultural dimensions of two famous authors: Hofstede and Hall. At first sight, the cultural dimensions of both researchers seem to differ extremely, but looking at them more closely, it becomes obvious that they are similar and even overlap partly. Even though these dimensions seem feasible, they are generally accepted and taught throughout the world, it is important to analyse their results critically, which will be the focus of the second part.

3.1 Hofstede and his Dimensions of Culture

Geert Hofstede, born in Haarlem, Netherlands, is probably the most widely known expert in cross-cultural research. Hofstede was eager to find out in which way values at one's workplace are influenced by culture. His analysis, which is the most frequently cited and probably one of the most comprehensive in this field, is based on the assumption that people are confronted with the same

Fig. 3: Geert Hofstede

problems (e.g. attitude towards authority), but act differently depending on their culture. From 1967 to 1973, while working at IBM as a psychologist in the Human Resources department, Hofstede collected and analysed data based on quantitative questionnaires completed by more than 100,000 individuals living in over 50 countries around the world. The questions were focused on work-related values, using 32 items to measure the importance of various work goals. Hofstede's work was published in his book *Cultures and Organizations: Software of the Mind* (1991), which, besides the original English version, has been translated into 16 other languages. Based on these results, and later additions, Hofstede developed a model that identifies four primary dimensions to differentiate cultures: Power Distance, Individualism vs. Collectivism,

Femininity vs. Masculinity and Uncertainty avoidance. He later added a fifth dimension: Long vs. Short-Term Orientation, which mainly focuses on Asian countries and is therefore not relevant for this thesis. Hofstede, 1997; Pateau, 1999

3.1.1 Power Distance

According to Hofstede (1997), *Power Distance* can be defined as "the extent to which the less powerful members of institutions and organizations within a country expect and accept that power is distributed unequally" (p. 28). Power Distance is therefore based on how inequality is handled within a country's society. Hofstede's survey contained three questions relating to power and inequality to be able to calculate the Power Distance Index (PDI) from the mean score of the standard sample of IBM employees. First, the employees were asked how often they had been afraid of criticising their superiors. Secondly, the interviewed persons were requested to characterise the current management style of their bosses (autocratic, paternalistic, and consultative) and, thirdly, which decision-making style of their superiors they would prefer. Interestingly, this analysis showed that the respondents' perception of the current decision-making style of their bosses corresponded to the decision-making style they favoured. As a result of his findings, Hofstede differentiates between Large and Small Power Distance countries. With a relatively high PDI score of 68, France belongs to the *Large Power Distance* countries. These countries are more dependent on supervision than Small Power Distance countries with a low PDI score. Employees of Large Power Distance countries expect autocratic decisions from their supervisors and often have difficulties in making decisions on their own. Moreover, they appreciate warm, paternal relationships with their superiors, even if there is a large distance of power involved. Germany, with a PDI score of 35, belongs to the *Small Power Distance* countries where employees expect more participation in questions concerning not only their job, but also company policy and strategy. Consequently, not an autocratic but rather a participative decision-making style is being applied. In contrast to Large Power Distance countries, people in Small Power Distance countries expect little direct supervision concerning their duties and prefer consultation, if at all. Since the emotional distance between workers and superiors is very small, employees approach and criticize their bosses more easily. Hofstede, 1997; Scarborough, 1998

3.1.2 Individualism vs. Collectivism

There are societies in which family ties and belonging to a group are considered more important than in other ones. Consequently, whether people feel they should take care of their families or the groups they belong to, can vary from society to society. Based on this assumption, Hofstede distinguishes between *individualist* and *collectivist* countries. *Individualism* focuses on the importance of the single person rather than the group (Collectivism), i.e. to which extent personal achievement is valued higher than collective achievement. Based on the results of his IBM analysis, Hofstede calculated the Individualism Index Score, which is high for individualist societies and low for collectivist societies.

Individualistic cultures, like the US (highest score), France (10th rank) as well as Germany (15th rank) belong to "societies in which the ties between individuals are loose" (Hofstede, 1997, p. 51). These people are more self-centred and put more emphasis on their individual goals and interests. They prefer straightforwardness and honesty in their conversations; even confrontations are regarded as positive. Individualistic societies prefer privacy and their duties (at work) often prevail over relationships.

Collectivist cultures, like most of the Asian countries are "societies in which people from birth onwards are integrated into strong, cohesive in-groups" (Hofstede, 1997, p. 51). Since children in collectivist cultures usually grow up among several elders, they are seldom alone and therefore see themselves "as part of a ´we´" (Hofstede, 1997, p. 58). Moreover, children raised in collectivist families are taught to agree with the group opinion, rather than develop their own ideas; an educational method practiced at school and in families of individualistic societies. Family celebrations, like marriages or baptisms are very important for collectivist societies. This might easily result in a confrontation with an individualistic boss, who would probably not understand why one of his employees comes late for an important meeting due to a family festivity. Hofstede, 1997

3.1.3 Femininity vs. Masculinity

In *masculine* societies emotional gender roles are clearly defined: "men are supposed to be assertive, tough, and focused on material success, whereas women are supposed to be more modest, tender, and concerned with the quality of life" (Hofstede, 1997, p. 82). Based on this fact, Hofstede differentiates between *masculine* countries, which are rather task-oriented and highly male-dominated and *feminine* countries, which attach great importance to strong relationships. The Masculinity Index determines whether a country is masculine (high score) or feminine (low score). The discrepancy between these two types of societies can also be noticed in connection with job 'segregation'. In masculine societies, like the US and Germany, the majority of teachers at grade and high school are women, whereas most of the lecturers at university are men. The same is true for business where men and not women usually hold higher-ranking positions. In feminine societies, like France and Denmark, roles are more equally divided and working mothers are given extra support with their children; these cultures prefer to solve conflicts by negotiation and compromise, rather than by confrontation. Furthermore, in feminine cultures modesty and solidarity are greatly respected, whereas masculine countries set high values on ambition, competition and results. Summing up, it may be said that members of feminine societies work to live but not live to work. Hofstede, 1997; Scarborough, 1998

3.1.4 Uncertainty Avoidance

The fourth dimension of Hofstede: *Uncertainty Avoidance* measures "the extent to which the members of a culture feel threatened by uncertain or unknown situations" (Hofstede, 1997, p. 113). Strong uncertainty might be caused by technology or nature and creates intolerable anxiety. This perception leads to extreme stress, which is also expressed in a need for predictability in written or unwritten rules. Human society has therefore developed several ways to explain and prevent uncertainties, like religion or laws. The Uncertainty Avoidance Index classifies cultures depending on how well they deal with uncertainty. A high score signifies a Strong Uncertainty Avoidance. Both, Germany (with a score of 65/100) and France (86/100), belong to the countries with a Strong Uncertainty Avoidance. Rules and regulations in private as well as in business life are binding for each individual. Strong uncertainty also entails looking for familiar solutions rather than innovative ones and a preference for structures (Scarborough, 1998). Unclear situations can cause disorientation and aggression. Accordingly, complex control systems are being established and violations are punished. In countries like Sweden, Denmark or the US, the Uncertainty Avoidance is rather weak. Their population appears to be easy going since people keep calm even in unclear or chaotic situations. Rules and regulations, which are only established if there is absolute necessity, are often ignored; control systems are flexible. Hofstede, 1997; Thomas, Kinas & Schroll-Machl, 2003

3.2 Hall's Dimensions of Culture

Fig. 4: Edward T. Hall

Another famous author dealing with intercultural dimensions is Edward T. Hall, an American anthropologist, also known as the founder of intercultural communication study (Sorrells, 1998). Based on his experience in the Foreign Service, Edward T. Hall published several books, "The Silent Language" (1959), "The Hidden Dimension" (1969), and „Beyond Culture" (1976), which focus on diverse types of communication (Hecht-El Minshawi, 2003). In order to prove their theories, Edward T. Hall and his wife, Mildred Reed Hall, (1990) questioned 180 employed persons using in-depth, open-ended interviews. The key factors of his theory are context, time and space.

3.2.1 High Context vs. Low Context

The term *context* includes the circumstances, information and conditions, which 'surround' an event. In communication, this term refers to the meaning of a statement, its connection to other parts of the message, the environment in which the communication takes place, and the perception of the receiver (Wikipedia, 05/2005). Context can be influenced by culture; for this reason Hall distinguishes in his studies between two different types of culture: *High* and *Low Context* cultures. Individuals belonging to *High Context* cultures are more likely to transmit information in non-verbal and indirect ways. "Japanese, Arabs, and Mediterranean people, who have extensive information networks among families, friends, colleagues and clients and who are involved in close personal relationships, are high-context" (Hall, 1990, p. 6). For people of these cultures, personal relationships are more important than anything else. They tend to be well informed on many subjects due to their extensive network, which enables a fast and spontaneous exchange of information. Moreover, words are of much less importance than the context, such as the speaker's intonation, facial expression or body language. Listeners need to be very attentive, since important facts are hidden 'between the lines'. Flowery language as well as lavish excuses is typical for high context cultures, like the French.

Americans, Germans, Swiss, Scandinavians and other Northern European countries belong to the *Low Context* culture. Unlike in High Context cultures, information in Low

Context cultures is shared only between particular individuals. Consequently, these people lack thorough and extensive information networks and therefore require or even anticipate a great deal of detailed background information. It seems obvious that this difference between cultures concerning the amount of context needed may entail several problems. Usually, High Context people become impatient and irritated when Low Context people provide them with very detailed information (Hall, 1990). In contrast, Low Context people feel lost if they do not receive enough information from their counterpart. Therefore, finding out the appropriate level of context is a big challenge. Hall 1990

3.2.2 Space

In his second dimension, Hall focuses on the concept of *space*. In this connection, he refers to one's attitude towards possession (territoriality) and the relationship towards other people (personal space), which are both "highly developed and strongly influenced by culture" (Hall, 1990, p. 10).

Territoriality is closely related to one's own possession, representing a high status for certain cultures. The cliché of all Germans washing their cars on weekends shows how much importance they attach to their property – you better not touch it as well. Moreover, German children often have their bed room door closed whenever they do not want to be disturbed which is not that usual in other countries. In German companies, *space* communicates power, symbolised by the top-floors being reserved for high-ranking managers, whereas French executives have their offices in the middle of their inferiors. They prefer being located centrally in order to be able to communicate and to be informed about everything that is happening around them.

Concerning *personal space*, a certain distance in space is common between individuals in Northern Europe, without it, people feel uncomfortable or pushed. Neighbours, for example, do not necessarily communicate with each other, unlike in America, where neighbourhood implicates a closer relationship and friendship. In contrast, in France as well as in most other High Context cultures, a person's bubble is smaller; touching somebody during a conversation is nothing unusual. If Germans, who belong to the Low Context cultures, sometimes appear cool, their reaction might be the result of someone having violated their personal space.

3.2.3 Time

The third dimension of Hall's studies takes into account the notion of *time*, which is closely connected to his previously mentioned dimension of *context*. In this connection, Hall differentiates between *monochronic* and *polychronic* societies. Monochronic societies are low-context and prefer to do one thing at a time, whereas high context polychronic societies do not mind doing several things simultaneously.

Members belonging to *monochronic societies* have a linear time perception. They are action-oriented, i.e. they do not like to be interrupted when concentrating on a certain task, and consequently are also concerned about not disturbing others. Furthermore, they take duties seriously and love to fix time commitments, such as deadlines or schedules. People of monochronic societies appreciate efficiency, promptness and adhere to rules. They are highly committed to their jobs and therefore often disregard interpersonal relationships. Typical examples for monochronic cultures are the US, Switzerland, Germany and the Scandinavian countries.

Polychronic societies, like France and other Southern countries, tend to have a rather cyclic time perception. They attach more importance to relationships (leading to a higher degree of context), rather than to punctuality or schedules, because they consider building social relationships part of doing business (Scarborough, 1998). Time is regarded as plentiful and being late is considered normal. Schedules should be adhered to if possible; interruptions occur frequently.

The connection between *time* and *space* becomes apparent when looking at German offices: closed doors are a typical example for monochronic cultures. Since people of these cultures are more action-oriented and not so much relationship-oriented, they think they can work more efficiently without being disturbed. Polychronic people do not like closed doors, they feel shut off from the flow of information. Naturally, these different time perceptions can be very frustrating for a monochronic person having a meeting with a polychronic person who is late and keeps answering the phone during their conversation. Hall 1990

3.3 Comparison of the two Models

When reading Geert Hofstede's book about cultural dimensions, his theory appears to be quite plausible. This is probably one of the reasons why his work has become very famous worldwide – and was met with great response especially among international business people. The same applies to the work of the researcher Edward T. Hall.

Although his approach was completely different from that of Hofstede, he also discovered cultural dimensions. Nevertheless, both authors have to resist criticism regarding their cultural findings. Thomas, Kinast & Schroll-Machl, 2003

3.3.1 Critical Observation of Hofstede's Dimensions

The empirical validity of Hofstede's framework has been extensively criticized in cross-cultural literature, since closer examination reveals that his theory is based on mere assumptions (Shackleton & Ali, 1990; Yoo & Donthu, 1998).

First of all, Hofstede draws conclusions from his questionnaires on an entire national population, which implies the danger of stereotyping. The interviewees (his sample) were simply employees in the subsidiaries of *one* large multinational company: IBM. There are no reasons for assuming that the average IBM responses reflect the national average, especially since the IBM culture is not representative of one nation. In favour of this argument are the company's exclusive recruitment from the 'middle class'; predominantly international training of employees, internationally centralised control and the relatively young age of its managers.

Moreover, it is argued that Hofstede denies the existence of cultural distinctions between inhabitants living in the same country. His dimensions exclude the coexistence of e.g. Individualism and Collectivism; although people's behaviour at home may differ considerably from their activities at work. In fact, the IBM data was restricted to the workplace and can therefore not be taken to describe or even measure the overall culture of a country. In addition, the questionnaire was influenced by Hofstede's own culture and his dimensions may be the result of the period in which the study was conducted. Nevertheless, Hofstede's model is generally accepted as the most comprehensive framework of national cultural values. Hofstede's dimensions have been considered valid, reliable and stable since their publication. Yoo & Donthu, 1998; McSweeney, 2002

3.3.2 Critical Observation of Hall's Framework

In contrast to the quantitative research of Hofstede, Hall tries to validate his assumptions by a more intuitional approach (see 3.2.1 - 3.2.3). Hall tries to avoid stereotyping throughout his thesis. Although he reassigns certain cultures to monochron or polychron societies (see 3.2.3), he states that one has to differentiate between business and private life. He cites the example of the US, whose inhabitants display an extremely monochron behaviour at work. In contrast, American

housewives can rather be assigned polychron, since they have to do multiple chores simultaneously. Hall suggests further, that, in general, women are rather polychron whereas men are monochron. Therefore, women have a high preference for relationships whereas men strive for individuality. As a result, women suffer from depression three to six times more often than men. In addition, Hall remarks that although French people are intellectually monochron, they exhibit polychron behaviour. These revelations show how difficult it is for Hall to make general statements about a certain culture. Furthermore, it may be criticised that Hall cites historical reasons for the development of cultural dimensions without further analysis.
Pateau, 1999

Hall's dimensions have found widespread acceptance being one of the most important research works in this field. His findings are an important tool for understanding the intercultural differences between Germans and French.

4 Germany and France

Although France and Germany share the same borders, there are a lot of things not known about 'the neighbour'. Being not familiar with the other culture and country may cause severe problems in business life. As a manager, it is therefore very important to be informed about the other culture (Breuer & de Bartha 2002).

The German as well as the French culture cannot be explained in a few sentences; an interdisciplinary approach is advisable (Fischer, 1996), since a culture is developed by a country's history, economy and society. But before analysing a foreign culture, it is important to first know and understand one's own country and civilisation. In view of this, a general picture of Germany and France will be provided throughout the following parts.

4.1 Germany

Since 1949, Germany's political system has been a parliamentary democracy consisting of 16 federal states with its central government located in Berlin.

The population density of Germany (82 Mio. inhabitants) is considerably higher than in France (Grosse & Lüger, 1994). As far as the religious affiliation is concerned, most Germans are Christians (33% Catholic, 33% protestant); a lower percentage belongs to Muslim or Jewish denominations (www.deutschland.de, 05/05). Although these facts about Germany are generally known they provide the basis for a comparison with France. What might be new and more interesting is what the French people associate with the Germans. A French woman working in a German-French corporation had a very positive impression of the Germans: "Très bonne, les Allemands sont plus ouverts et indépendants que les Francais"[7]. In contrast, the Sales manager of OSRAM / Molsheim characterized the Germans as "gens rigoureux"[8]. Evidently, there are varying perceptions of Germans, sometimes positive and sometimes negative. Where do these different images of the German society result from? The examination of the history and society in the following parts might provide further explanation. In this connection, it is important to mention that the analysis does not claim integrity nor does it over or undervalue certain aspects. The

---

[7] *Suggested translation by the author:* "Very good, Germans are more open-minded and independent than the French."

[8] *Suggested translation by the author:* "strict people"

main emphasis is on the relation between environmental circumstances and the resulting developed behaviour.

4.1.1 Historical Background

A fundamental characteristic of Germany and its history is federal structure and lack of central authority. In France, Philipp II August was able to consolidate royal domination as early as the beginning of the 13th century, whereas in Germany the power rested with the secular and clerical *Territorialherren*. Although a king was elected, power over the armed forces was assigned to the sovereigns and the papacy. The fragmentation process was strengthened by the baronial sovereignty and up to the 17th century, the *Heilige Römische Reich Deutscher Nationen* was nothing but an alliance of sovereign states, held together by the imperial crown. There was no basis for a centralistic form of government. The Franco-Prussian war in 1870/71 softened the sectionalism, and finally – somewhat later than France, Spain and England – a united country with national consciousness and pride emerged. Despite this development, Germany has always had a federal system governed by the individual interests of the member states, with the exception of the national socialist regime.

Furthermore, Luther's reformation, which took place in the 16th century, had a great impact on Germany's population. During several battles and wars, protestant adherents struggled with their catholic opponents. In the peace of Augsburg (1555) every German state was granted the right to decide between Lutheranism and Catholicism (Wikipedia, 05/05).

Germany's recent history was strongly affected by two devastating world wars in the first half of the 20th century. By the end of the Second World War (1945) Germany was left occupied by the victorious Allied powers of the US, UK, France, and the Soviet Union. In 1949, the Cold War separated Germany into two parts: the Western Federal Republic of Germany (FRG) and the Eastern German Democratic Republic (GDR). The decline of the USSR and the end of the Cold War cleared the path for German reunification in 1990 (Wikipedia, 05/05). In January 1999, Germany and ten other EU countries introduced a common European currency, the Euro.

Today, the collective mind of the majority of the German population is still dominated by the national socialist dictatorship during World War II. The Germans are coined very strongly by this catastrophe and therefore have a gap in their history, which is extremely difficult to deal with. This is probably one of the main reasons why, even the younger generation of Germans shows less national pride than other nationalities (Stiftung Haus der Geschichte, 1998). Scarborough, 1998; Grosse & Lüger, 1994

4.1.2 Culture and Society

Germans sometimes appear to be stiff and unfriendly at first sight. Since they prefer lengthy discussions with close friends to small talk (Lewis, 1999), it will take some time until one is considered a 'real friend' of a German. But once 'the ice is broken', Germans are quite frank and even talk about their deepest feelings. In general, friendships are highly appreciated in Germany, and being invited to one's home is a real honour (Hall, 1990).

Moreover, Germans are task as well as goal-oriented. They belong to the *low context* cultures (see 3.2.1). Germans strive for equality (see 3.1.1) and are rather consensus-oriented. They are *individualistic* (see 3.1.2) and belong to *masculine* rather than *feminine* societies (see 3.1.3). Germans favour rules and laws, which give them orientation and security (Scarborough, 1998). Although, they often hide their feelings, Germans seem to have no problems in expressing criticism openly. Germans are known for high quality products as well as for working efficiently. Its inhabitants seek approval and have a distinct sense of duty for contributing to the public welfare. Consequently, Germans often participate in foundations for public utility (Breuer & de Bartha, 2002). Time is very important for German people – they love to plan and to adhere to schedules; promptness is taken for granted (Hecht-El Minshawi, 2003). In addition, many Germans of today attach great importance to their family life as well as to leisure time. Adventurous spare time activities, like bungee jumping, seem to be a compensation for ambition and perfection shown during work. Breuer & de Bartha, 2002

Concerning the society, the importance of church and religion represents probably the greatest difference compared to France or other countries. Although, church and state have been separated since 1919 (Wikipedia, 05/05), and interest in religion – especially of the younger generation – is decreasing, religious institutions still play an important role in Germany. Since the beginning of the 19th century, the State collects church taxes from every employed person belonging to a religious denomination. Their representatives exert great influence on public life, in particular in rural areas and are, in addition, involved in the political parties. Grosse & Lüger, 1994

4.1.3 Education System

Since the sovereignty of the 16 federal states constitutes the main element of national education, there has never been a unified national education system in Germany. Common rules have been introduced in order to create general regulations and guarantee mobility between the federal states, but there are still no standardised syllabuses. Germany is eager to compensate the weaknesses of its system, but so far the Conference of the State Ministries of Education has only served as counterbalance to the decision-making federal states. In the course of growing international and European integration, Germany and the federal states will have to make adjustments in order to correspond to international standards (Picht & Kolle, 2005).

Looking at the education system itself, German children start attending *Kindergarten* at the age of three on a voluntary basis. The main functions of these institutions are to conciliate, look after, cultivate and educate. After this period, children pass on to the *Grundschule* for the next four years in which they are prepared for further education. Before entering the 5th grade, the decision has to be made which institution to choose next, the *Hauptschule*, *Realschule* or the *Gymnasium*. Only the last one enables to qualify for university studies. Depending on the federal states where they live and under certain circumstances, children attending the *Hauptschule* or *Realschule* also have the possibility of studying at a university.

The weakest link in the German school system is the *Hauptschule* because the number of German students declines, whereas the number of foreigners increases. Therefore an adequate education is often not possible.

"Within the German education system, the concept of *Bildung* still predominantly implies 'self-maturation'. The educator only gives the 'plant', the evolving personality, support. It can only develop and learn about itself by means of its character, decisions and commitment to its studies" (Grosse & Lüger, 1994, p. 215).

Due to the influence of the church on society, as already mentioned, religion is usually taught at every German school; theology is traditionally offered as a major at universities. Furthermore, two-thirds of all kindergartens are managed and fully or partly financed, by either the Protestant or the Catholic Church. Grosse & Lüger, 1994

4.1.4 Economy

In the second half of 19th century, Germany went through a heavy industrialization period. "By 1900 there were already more people working in the secondary than in the primary sector" (Grosse & Lüger, 1994, p. 143). Due to the rapid population growth, the industrialization process was much more developed than in France at that time. Germany became a technologically strong economy belonging once to the third largest national economies in the world.

Nowadays, however, it has turned into one of the slowest growing economies in Europe. The current growth of the GDP (2004) is extremely low (+1.7%) and a quick turnaround is not foreseeable (www.deutschland.de, 05/05). Reasons for this slow growth are the costly process of reintegrating the Eastern German economy ($70 billion per year), Germany's aging population and the high unemployment rate (11.5%) (Statistisches Bundesamt Deutschland, 08/05). Due to strict labour market regulations, unemployment has become a big problem in Germany, especially in the East ('East-West divide'). Structural reforms, as well as corporate restructuring and growing capital markets are necessary for Germany to overcome the current slow growth. In the short run, however, decreasing government revenues and rising expenditures will continue to raise the deficit above the EU's debt limit (CIA World Fact book, 05/05).

Although the present economic situation in Germany is difficult, the exports still constitute an important part of the country's revenue. Taking a closer look, it can be noticed that France is the main consumer of German goods and services (24%), followed by the Netherlands (22%), USA (20%), Great Britain (17%) and Italy (17%).

The *Deutscher Gewerkschaftsbund* (Confederation of German Trade Unions), which was formed after World War II, exercises a great influence on decisions concerning employment and wages. This federation, which is "more geared towards the mediation of opposing interests than in France" (Grosse & Lüger, 1994, p. 205), combines a number of unions and represents the majority of all union members.
Grosse & Lüger, 1994

4.2 France

"Ein echter Mann mag keine Franzosen leiden, doch ihre Weine trinkt er gern."[9] This saying by Johann Wolfgang von Goethe (Stiftung Haus der Geschichte, 1998) clearly characterises the attitude of a lot of Germans towards their French neighbours. During the interviews, which were conducted for this thesis, several words appeared frequently when Germans were asked to describe their impressions of the French: savoir-vivre, laissez faire, open-minded people, patriotism, strikes, etc. Many of these positive remarks result from the fact that France is considered a holiday country.

France is not only a tourist region, but also the largest country of the European Union, with a surface area of 551,000 square kilometres (Fischer, 1991). It is divided in 26 regions; 22 in the mother country itself and four overseas departments. Since the overseas departments are influenced by the local cultures and do not fully represent the French culture, this research will only examine the mainland of France.

France has 58.5 million inhabitants (Fischer Weltalmanach, 2004), 82% of which are Catholics (www.spiegel.de, 03/05). Half of the population is living in urban centres; Paris city with 2.1 million (and the metropolitan area of Paris with 10.8 million inhabitants) being the most populous city (Auswärtiges Amt, 08/05; Grosse & Lüger, 1994). Sometimes entrepreneurs ask themselves if it is really necessary to choose Paris as a location for their company. But the question probably needs to be reversed: can a company afford not to open a branch in Paris? (Herterich, 1991) Paris is the centre of France and demonstrates the strong centralisation of the country. Most of the public authorities, institutions, national and international organisations, as well as most banks, companies and media are located in Paris (Herterich, 1991). Moreover the centralisation affects modern politics. Planning and decision-making affecting even the remotest areas of the country are made in the capital (Grosse & Lüger, 1994).

The purpose of the next chapter is not to provide a detailed analysis of the French history, but to give a short overview of the most important events, followed by an extract about French culture and society, its education system and economical development.

---

[9] *Suggested translation by the author:* "A real man does not like French people, but likes drinking their wine."

4.2.1 Historical Background

"Liberté, Fraternité et Egalité"[10] - everyone will associate these keywords with the *French Revolution* which took place in 1789. As a consequence, the French Republic was set up in 1792 and the modern state of France developed faster and more intensified (Lüsebrink, 2000). About a century later (1870), one of the most important events between Germany and France took place: the Franco-Prussian War. Further details will be provided in chapter 5.1.1.

The French history is coined by two important aspects, which originated from two different periods and have had a decisive influence in making France what it is today. The first one is *centralisation* of the state and the concentration of the governmental power in Paris (Lüsebrink, 2000). In contrast to Germany, the development of France was dedicated to centralise all federal powers and to avert separatism, despite various efforts to decentralise the country. The principles of national unity date back to the absolute monarchy of Louis XIV (1643-1715). "Looking back at French history, one can see that efforts towards national unity and towards building up a strong centralistic oriented system of government played a predominant role in all time periods" (Grosse & Lüger, 1994, p. 11).

The second one is the *autocratic* character of the French *government*. The president has a very dominating position whereas the parliament only plays a subordinate role. This feature originated from the constitution of the 5th Republic, when France was at colonial war with Algeria and suffered a serious domestic crisis. Charles de Gaulle, French president at the time, considered the strengthening of his position as a central element to overcome the crisis and instability resulting from numerous changes of governance (Lüsebrink, 2000). "Obviously rigid administrative centralism of this kind left little room for autonomy or regional initiative" (Grosse & Lüger, 1994, p. 3). As a result, there has been little motivation for the population to be actively involved in politics. Furthermore, the present French government is frequently associated with a population resisting any form of governmental authority.

The recent history (following the *Liberation* in 1950) was conditioned by economic reconstruction and a change in industrial orientation. Besides, the colonial issue (wars in Indochina and Algeria) resulted in a loss of the colonies. Grosse & Lüger, 1994

---

[10] *Suggested translation by the author:* "Freedom, Fraternity and Equality."

4.2.2 Culture and Society

French people are very proud of their nation and history, which is famous for powerful heroes like Henry IV, Napoleon or Louis XIV as well as the vast achievements of the Renaissance and the Revolution. Numerous statues and monuments have been erected in villages and cities to commemorate these glorious leaders. Scarborough, 1998

The national pride of the French, their great history, as well as their beautiful landscape, are certainly not stimulating to learn foreign languages. French prefer foreigners to speak their language and they can get annoyed if this is not the case (Hall, 1990). Indeed, the generation of today has recognized the importance of learning and speaking other languages.

Due to the previously mentioned colonial wars, many subcultures from North Africa and other Mediterranean countries can be found in France. These cultures have exerted an additional Latin influence on the French population. This might be a reason why French people cannot be explicitly assigned to *low* or *high context* cultures (see 3.2.1). According to Hofstede, they are not averse to a great distance between individuals concerning power (see 3.1.1). French people have a distinct *uncertainty avoidance* (see 3.1.4) and can be described as *individualistic* (see 3.1.2) as well as *feminine* (see 3.1.3). Hecht-El Minshawi, 2003

Power, originality and admiration are key values for French people, who love change and challenge (Breuer & de Bartha, 2002). French people do not like to stick to plans and schedules; they attach more importance to relationships than to appointments. Their theme of the day is to enjoy life: e.g. French people attach great importance to good food and wine as well as to long meals with friends or family. In addition, they have a laid-back attitude and do not persist on details but on the general view of a task. Hall, 1990

French families set high value on common activities, traditions and parental authority. In contrast to Germany, the double role of women is commonly accepted in society and the compatibility of family and work is supported by family-friendly politics (Lüsebrink, 2003). Consequently, in France, the ratio for working mothers (50%) is considerably higher than in Germany (35%) (Grosse & Lüger, 1994).

Due to the complete separation of state and church (1905), religious affiliation as well as prayers and church attendance are not very prevalent in France. Lüsebrink, 2003

4.2.3 Education System

The education system in France has undergone a step-by-step centralization process in the 19th century. "The level of the baccalaureat is standardized throughout France due to the fact that the exam is centrally administered" (Grosse & Lüger, 1994, p. 218). Since state and church are fully separated, two different types of school systems exist: the public school system (*école publique*), which does not provide any religious instruction and the private school system (*école privée*). French children start their school life with the *école maternelle*, which has a considerably higher attendance rate than in Germany (52% of the two-year-old children and 100% of the three-year-old children visit this institution). French parents are convinced that their children should live together with peers from their earliest childhood, whereas German parents (also due to the shortage of day-nurseries) prefer to keep their little ones at home a few months longer (Lüsebrink, 2000). *Ecoles maternelles* are considered part of the school system, which is the reason why – unlike in Germany – its teachers are trained and paid like normal teachers. The *école primaire* is, just as the German *Grundschule,* the preliminary stage to *collège*. In contrast to the German children, who have to decide relatively early which school they want to attend, the French childrens´ choice is delayed until they finish *collège*. After that, they have the possibility of entering an *apprentissage*, three-years of *lycée* or two-years of *lycée professionnel*. French children attend all-day schools from *école maternelle* up to *lycée*, thus they are accustomed to full-time school life at a very young age. The *baccalauréat*, the final exam passed at *lycées*, allows entering university. French universities, which are separated into the *Grandes Ecoles*, universities as well as universities with a stronger focus on practical experience, attract more students than in Germany; consequently, the quality of education suffers. The university system in France is characterised by the outstanding reputation of the *Grandes Ecoles*. These 'elitist' universities have gained great importance since the majority of French in leading positions in nearly all fields (administration, politics, technology, trade and commerce) have graduated from there.

Generally, it can be said that the concept of the French education system is based on a less individualistic approach than in Germany and attaches great importance to their language and the knowledge of national history (Lewis, 1999). Grosse & Lüger, 1994

4.2.4 Economy

In the 19th century, France was mainly an agricultural country. At that time, approximately 45 to 50% of its workforce was engaged in farming, the industrialization process was progressing slowly, and the overall economic growth was at a low level. Grosse & Lüger, 1994

"Starting in 1945, France went trough an industrialization process which had taken over 100 years in Germany" (Grosse & Lüger, 1994, p. 153). This development brought radical changes to the predominantly agrarian country. The percentage of workers employed in the primary sector dropped drastically (50% between 1946 and 1962); this decline was beneficial for industry and services. In addition, this development was accompanied by the migration of farm workers into urban centres. This movement, encouraged by better job offers, did not result in urbanisation but in a population increase of some economic centres (e.g. Paris, Lyon and Marseille). The development of Paris as the most important city of France does not only have a positive impact on the economy, it also entails immense transportation, housing and environmental problems, as well as impairing the economy of other regions. After 1945, the French economy was mainly focused on reconstruction and the opening towards European countries, which resulted in a faster growth and modernisation (Lüsebrink, 2003).

Generally, it can be observed, that there is a high degree of governmental influence on the French economic system. Although many large companies, banks, and insurers have been fully or partially privatised, the government still controls parts of several leading firms, like Air France, France Telecom and Renault. Moreover, it plays a predominant role in several public sectors like power, public transport, and defence industries. Grosse & Lüger, 1994

Today, the French economy is growing slowly with a GDP of 1.9% (agriculture: 4%, industry: 25%, services: 71%) and an unemployment rate of 10% (Tradeport, 08/05). The main exporting countries are: Germany (14%), Great Britain (10%), Spain (10%), Italy (9%) and the United States with 7%. Fischer Weltalmanach, 2001

The representation of professional interests, as well as participation in labour unions, is not very high. Due to this fact, strikes have priority over negotiations (Grosse & Lüger, 1994). Differing from the general perception, the frequency of strikes in France is higher than in Germany, but lower than in other countries like Italy or Great Britain. The general impression of a higher strike frequency in France is due to the fact that they occur mainly in the public sector (railway, aviation and post) and therefore paralyse the public life. Lüsebrink, 2003

5 The Approach of Germany and France in Everyday Life and Business

5.1 Development of the Relationship between Germany and France

On the occasion of the 40th anniversary of the Elysée Treaty (2003), which provided the basis for the cooperation between Germany and France, Mr. Fischer, the German minister of foreign affairs, pointed out the importance of this treaty for the European Union: "Die deutsch-französische Zusammenarbeit ist der Kern und das Schwungrad der europäischen Entwicklung gewesen und wird dies

Fig. 5: 40th Anniversary -Elysée Treaty

[...] auch unter den Bedingungen der EU der 25 bleiben"[11] (Auswärtiges Amt, 2003). Germany and France have been considered as the impulsive forces of the European Union over the last twenty years (Deutsche Bundesregierung, 05/2005).

In order to find out what the Germans think about their neighbours, the German newspaper *Die Zeit* published an opinion poll. The results were positive, but contradictory: the Germans consider the French population as cordial and associate such things as beautiful landscapes, Paris, the Eiffel tower, as well as magnificent holiday resorts. Although 80% of the Germans regard the French as nationalists, 72% describe them as open-minded and in favour of a unified Europe. The general opinion of the French about Germans is less optimistic. Less and less French people are interested in Germany, a phenomenon that can be noticed primarily among young people. Even if they study German as their first foreign language at school, they are more attracted by the Anglo-Saxon world across the Atlantic than by their German-speaking neighbours. Ecoute, 2000

As the intercultural relationship between France and Germany is the result of a long history full of tensions, its current situation can only be understood by the knowledge of their common history; this will be further discussed in the following section (Zimmermann, 1995).

---

[11] *Suggested translation by the author:* "The German-French cooperation has been the core and the impulse of the development of Europe and will even take this part under the conditions of the European Union of the 25."

5.1.1 Historical Development of the Bilateral Relations

In the 18th century, France was of great interest to Germans because they visited the neighbouring country to learn French manners and observe generally accepted forms of behaviour. In contrast to the Germans, which had been travelling to France for several centuries, the French intellectuals did not show any interest in Germany until after the French Revolution (1789). Zimmermann, 1995

After a period of peace, the German-French relationship was affected by war and distrust. The first event took place in 1870: the Franco-Prussian War. This conflict represented the peak of a period of alternating dominations between France and Germany in the 18th and 19th century. The main reasons for this war were the contrasts in political power between France and Prussia. This caused Napoleon III, emperor of France at that time, to declare war. Due to an underestimation of the power of the Prussian military, allied with the states of Southern Germany, France suffered a defeat and lost Alsace as well as the German-speaking section of Lorraine (Treaty of Frankfurt, 1871). Apart from the territorial and financial losses, the Franco-Prussian War meant a cut in the French-German relationship. Many French intellectuals revised their positive picture of Germany: "Der gute Deutsche wurde ersetzt durch den grausamen heuchlerischen Deutschen"[12] (Zimmermann, 1995, p. 128), as illustrated by the image on the right (Fig. 6).

Fig. 6: Voisins et Enemies (neighbours and enemies)

A 'cold war' developed between France and Germany, marked by a policy of revenge, which was the origin of the hereditary enemy thinking (Stiftung Haus der Geschichte, 1998) on the French side, and a military dictatorship in the regions of Alsace-Lorraine on the German side. While Germany formed an alliance with Austria and Italy (*Triple Alliance*), France formed the *Entente Cordiale* with Great Britain and later the *Triple Entente* with Great Britain and Russia. Due to this development, Germany became more and more encircled and isolated. This situation resulted in preparations for war and an intensification of nationalism among the German people. However, the event triggering off *World War I* (1914-18) was the assassination attempt in Sarajevo. Following this, the alliances fought a 'positional warfare', which ended with the battle

---

[12] *Suggested translation by the author:* "The nice German has been replaced by the cruel hypocritical German."

of Verdun, where the Germans were driven back by the French army. Finally the Germans surrendered to the French and signed an armistice agreement on November 11, 1918 (Stiftung Haus der Geschichte, 1998) followed by the *Treaty of Versailles*, which was imposed on Germany on June 28, 1919. This treaty had the major goal of changing Germany from a domineering, warlike and dangerous country, to a harmless nation. Since Germany was made responsible for the war, it had to pay enormous reparations. Alsace-Lorraine and some of Germany's African colonies were passed to France; in addition, France occupied the Rhineland and the Saarland. The treaty resulted in a wave of nationalism in Germany and poisoned the Franco-German relations for many years. Yet, the *Treaty of Locarno* (1925) represented an initial rapprochement between France and Germany, by treating various political questions through diplomatic channels and granting Germany a permanent seat in the League of Nations. Fischer, 1991

The peace ended on September 3, 1939, when France declared war on Germany because Germany had invaded Poland. This was the beginning of *World War II* (1939-45). In 1940, Hitler attacked France, Alsace-Lorraine was re-annexed to Germany, and France was divided into an occupied zone in the north and a clear zone in the south, also as the *Government de Vichy*. In 1942, Germany conquered the clear zone; France remained occupied until the Allies liberated it on August 25, 1944. Fischer, 1991

Although Germany and France were considered *hereditary enemies,* and the life of the French was dominated by great fear towards the brutal Germans, the attitude of the French versus the Germans changed a lot during post-war era (1945-49): France was no longer just an occupying power, but also a neighbour concerned about the future of the German people. Additionally, France offered its support for the reconstruction of Germany. The objective was to transform Germans into 'human beings' and to impose the French values of liberty, equality and fraternity. At that time, the first meetings between French and German young people took place. Slowly, the politicians got used to the new situation; an atmosphere of trust developed.

In 1958, *Charles de Gaulle* was elected president of the French Republic. His appointment was initially met with scepticism because de Gaulle personified a nationalistic rather than a European policy. In contrast, his first meeting with Germany's chancellor, *Konrad Adenauer,* on September 1958, was a success: the two politicians decided to establish "direct and preferential relationships" between

France and Germany, and to stay in "close personal contact" (Colard, 1999, p. 20). In July 1962, during de Gaulle's visit in Germany, *Adenauer* proposed drawing up a document defining the terms of the Franco-German cooperation, also known as the *Elysée Treaty* (Französische Botschaft, 2002) – the picture on the right emphasises the historically important event of French-German friendship. The treaty began with a common declaration of the two heads of state, insisting on reconciliation, solidarity and friendship. In the field of foreign policy, the two governments promised to consult each other on issues of common interest. Moreover, the treaty had a harmonising effect on the different defence strategies. In the domain of education and youth, the two states agreed on teaching the partner's language, adopting equivalences concerning exams, diplomas and titles, as well as collaborating in the field of scientific research.

Fig. 7: Reconciliation between Adenauer and the Gaulle

In the following years, the presidents as well as the German chancellors supported the reciprocal friendship by making various efforts to intensify the German-Franco relationship.

The fall of the Berlin Wall, on November 9, 1989, resulted in the reunification of East and West Germany. Although the growing strength of 'Big Germany' was regarded by part of the French population with some fear, the majority considered the event as positive from an economic point of view. They believed that a political union in Europe, induced by the opening of the market towards the East, could make it easier to control the potential danger of German supremacy. These thoughts led to the *Maastricht Treaty* in 1992, initiated by France and Germany, which transformed the European Community into the European Union (Colard, 1999). Stiftung Haus der Geschichte, 1998

Despite several crises (e.g. the resumption of the French nuclear tests in the South Pacific in 1995), the relationship between Germany and France nowadays has become very intense and amicable (Lüsebrink, 2003). The latest political developments will be considered in detail in the next chapter.

5.1.2 Political Relations

The political relations have been the starting point of the Franco-German friendship. Since the signing of the *Elysée Treaty*, three types of different political relations have developed: the intergovernmental, the parliamentary and the military relations. Last but not least, there is the collaboration in the field of foreign and security policy: *the program France / Franco-German relations*.

The *intergovernmental cooperation* consists of Franco-German consultations taking place twice a year involving organisations like the Franco-German defence council, the Franco-German economic council and the Franco-German environmental council. In addition, the two heads of state meet for informal talks every six or eight weeks. Auswärtiges Amt, 02/2005

The *parliamentary relations* include the annual meeting between the *Bundestag*, Germany's lower house of parliament, and the French National Assembly, as well as regular discussions between the members of the political parties. Auswärtiges Amt, 02/2005

The *military cooperation* includes the European corps, which originated from the *French-German Brigade* founded in 1989. The Franco-German initiative aroused the interest of other countries; nowadays, nearly all members of the European Union have joined this alliance. Eurocorps, 08/2005

The *program France / Franco-German relations* is the constant analysis of the bilateral relations between both countries. It was founded in 1989 within the German society for foreign policy (*Deutsche Gesellschaft für Auswärtige Politik e.V.*) and concentrates its efforts on aspects of foreign and security policy. Moreover, it participates in debates, research and plays an advisory role in economic and social areas in France. In addition, it acts as a mediator between France and Germany. DGAP, 08/2005

The preliminary highlight of a number of rapprochements between the two countries was the fact that Mr. Schröder was the first German chancellor to be invited to the ceremony commemorating the 60th anniversary of the disembarkment of the allied troops (D-day) in Normandy. This important gesture of sympathy made a particular impression on the younger generation (Auswärtiges Amt, 2/2005). The Iraq War of 2003 was another milestone, where France and Germany stood alongside against the war intentions of the US (Lüsebrink, 2003).

5.1.3 Economic Relations

"Die wirtschafliche Zusammenarbeit zwischen Deutschland und Frankreich ist in der Geschichte ohne Vorbild. Niemals zuvor haben zwei Länder enger und in größerem Umfang wirtschaftlich zusammengearbeitet."[13] (Herterich, 2000)

Since the end of the sixties, France and Germany have a profitable partnership, with high percentage of foreign trade between the two neighbouring countries. Germany is selling technical and consumer goods to France, whereas France is the leading exporter of high-grade agricultural goods as well as aerospace technology (Stiftung Haus der Geschichte, 1998). German products have gained a reputable position in the French economy, and a number of German companies have become market leaders within their respective industrial sectors (Herterich, 2000).

This trade relationship favours numerous business cooperations, financial institutions and all kind of trade organisations. In addition, there is close economic teamwork between the two states: permanent coordination and regular parliamentary exchange takes place on a bilateral basis as well as on European level. The tight linkage represents the basis for the common economic and monetary development within in the European Union, like e.g. the Euro.

Since the mutual trade is heavily 'interlocked', the economic trend of *one* country has immediate repercussions on the other country, either positive or negative ones. It may, on one hand, entail a growth of both economies, or result in an economic slowdown as well as rising unemployment. Despite this, numerous partnerships and businesses have been set up in the neighbour countries. There are several German businesses in France and vice-versa; most of the large corporations (Siemens, Bosch, Hoechst or BASF) have an affiliate located in the partner country. "Von 1988-1998 haben die deutschen Investitionen in Frankreich trotz der Wiedervereinigung gleichmäßig zugenommen und sich mehr als verdreifacht"[14] (Stiftung Haus der Geschichte, 1998, p. 138).

Globalisation and the European monetary union will lead to an increase of cooperations and the relevance of collaboration between the two cultures. However,

---

[13] *Suggested translation by the author:* "The economic cooperation between Germany and France has been without precedent in history. Never before has there been a closer and more extensive cooperation in the field of economy."

[14] *Suggested translation by the author:* "From 1988-1998, the German investments in France continously increased and even tripled, despite of the reunification."

German-French cooperations are often not desired due to psychological reasons and a different way of thinking. Stiftung Haus der Geschichte, 1998

5.1.4 Cultural Relations

Starting with the signing of the *Elysée Treaty* in the fifties, the network of social relationships between the two countries has become stronger and stronger.

Many initiatives have been taken in order to promote an intercultural exchange. One of the first was the *Comité Francais d´Echange avec l´Allemagne nouvelle,* which was founded in 1948. In the same year, the DFI (*Deutsch-Französisches Institut*) was founded with the goal of German-French agreement in all areas (Zimmermann, 1995). German-French magazines (e.g. *Dokumente-document*) were published to provide a better information flow. Numerous meetings and exchanges between German and French exports (jurists, scientists, and authors) were organized. The *Deutsch-Französische Jugendwerk* (*Office Franco-Allemand pour la Jeunesse*), which was founded in 1963, initiated exchange programmes for pupils and students, partnerships of schools, universities and sports clubs (Auswärtiges Amt, 2004). Since then, about seven million young Germans and French (every year over about 165,000) have participated in programs to promote intercultural understanding (www.deutschland-und-frankreich.de, 08/05). The aim of these programs is to abolish prejudices and facilitate intercultural understanding, especially among young people. In addition to these initiatives, the first German-French youth parliament (in October 1983), where roughly one hundred young Germans and French were having discussions with the deputies of both countries, took place.

In 1990, the contract for the foundation of the European culture channel *ARTE* was signed and the first transmissions were broadcasted in 1992 (Französische Botschaft, 12/2002). In October 2003, the first conference between the French regions and the German federal states was held in an effort to promote the regional collaboration.

The main pulse for the German-French cooperation, however, was released by the communities. A total of 2,200 town twinnings have contributed considerably to the rapprochement of both countries (www.deutschland-und-frankreich.de, 08/2005).

These strong relations on a social and cultural level represent the basis for an understanding of the other country. Thus, profound misunderstandings, which have occurred frequently in German-French history, may be avoided. Bundeszentrale für politische Bildung, 08/05

5.1.5 Cooperation in the Field of Education

"Trotz 40 Jahren deutsch-französischer Freundschaft gibt es noch immer viel Mißtrauen und viele Hindernisse, zu denen nicht zuletzt auch die mangelnde Kenntnis des anderen und die Verkennung seiner Kultur gehört, die bei der Unkenntnis seiner Sprache anfängt."[15] (Schäfer, H. et al, 1998, p. 140)

Language is an essential pre-requisite for intercultural communication. Unfortunately more and more students loose interest in their neighbour country and consequently, less and less Germans learn French and vice-versa.

In German schools this trend continues despite various efforts to arouse interest in the French language: French is frequently taught as a second language and first attempts have been introduced to teach the neighbouring language in elementary schools. As early as 1969, the first German-French bilingual courses were introduced in three federal states of Germany (Französische Botschaft, 12/2002). However, due to the fierce competition of English and Spanish, the French language is in danger of being displaced. Zimmermann, 1995

Student exchanges are another method of promoting the learning process of a foreign language and the corresponding culture. According to analyses of the DAAD (2003), student mobility between France and Germany is relatively stable. In 2001/02, 3,243 of 16,626 German (Erasmus/Socrates) students spent a semester in France (3,291 in Spain and 3,229 in the United Kingdom), whereas only 2,779 of 18,149 French (Erasmus/Socrates) students studied in Germany (Germany ranking third in the European Union after the UK: 5,052 and Spain: 3,893). As the graph on the right shows, the proportion of German students studying in France has decreased, but has stabilized at 30%, whereas the proportion of French students studying in Germany has slightly increased.

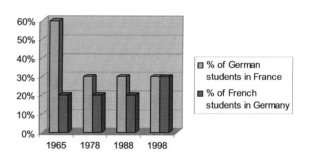

Fig. 8: The academic mobility between Germany and France

---

[15] *Suggested translation by the author:* "Despite of the 40-year relationship between Germany and France, there is still a lot of distrust and many obstacles, among them, last but not least, the missing knowledge of the other country as well as the misjudging of the other culture, beginning with the lack of knowledge of the other language."

5.2 Business Culture between French and German Companies

The management environment of today is in constant change; almost every day people are confronted with intercultural conflicts, sometimes without even noticing it. Although small internal conflicts may harm the working atmosphere or cause the failure of projects, the largest difficulties occur when a French company and a German company merge. There are several successful cooperations (e.g. the French insurance company *AGF* and the German *Allianz-Group*), others resulted in a collapse and immense costs (Breuer & de Bartha, 2002).

The main reasons for these failures are the highly differing core values of French and Germans. Core values are the result of attitudes formed by historical experience, geography, cultural relations, etc. (Lewis, 1999). The information given in the previous chapters will therefore be extremely helpful for understanding the core values and differing attitudes, which have repercussions on business life between the members of both cultures. Breuer and de Bartha (2002) have summed up these differences in one sentence "Deutsche wollen überzeugen - Franzosen verführt werden."[16] (p. 162). The next chapters will focus on dominant behaviour patterns concerning the handling of authority, work organization, interpersonal communication and keys for motivation, formed by the two cultures over the centuries.

Reading the next part, it must be kept in mind once again that there is no general truth considering French and German behaviour patterns. However, the following facts were derived from several *practical* experiences gathered by Breuer & de Bartha (2002).

5.2.1 Management Style

First of all, it is important to know that there is a difference between the German and the French perception of the term *management*.

In Germany, *management* denotes facilitating and systematising complex procedures. Furthermore, consensus-oriented decisions among all employees involved are preferred and regarded as efficient. In addition, superiors, in consensus with their employees, contribute to the advancement of processes in order to have everything under control and to avoid unforeseen events. Employees are expected to adhere to

---

[16] *Suggested translation by the author:* "Germans want to be convinced – French to be seduced."

these processes since they were decided by mutual consent.

In contrast, French employees seldom participate in the planning process. Superiors execute constant control and have an autocratic management style. In France, the dispositions of a respected boss replace written rules and assignments, which are common in Germany. For the French, *management* therefore means permanently controlling the employees' motivation. Pressurising, by setting earlier deadlines, is regarded as a common method. Breuer & de Bartha, 2002

The following chapter will therefore focus on the role of the superior and analyse how decisions are reached in both countries. Furthermore, knowledge about the core values of 'power' and 'money', which is important to avoid misunderstandings in business negotiations, will be disclosed.

5.2.1.1 The Role of the Boss

One of the interviewees referred to in Pateau's book "Die seltsame Alchimie in der Zusammenarbeit von Deutschen und Franzosen" (1999), mentioned that in France, superiors had a higher authority than in Germany. He further stated that many French bosses were less cooperative and much more paternalistic towards their employees and that in many corporations, hierarchy levels were more important than in Germany. In addition, the boss was not contradicted in front of others. Hofstede names this difference in equality *Power Distance* (see 3.1.1).

Looking back at French history, the correlation between authority and centralism (see 4.2.1) becomes obvious. Yet, in the 17th and 18th century, every form of motivation of the lower-ranking population to actively participate was restrained by the monarchs´ urban and fiscal policy. Since the centralisation process has continued until today, collective actions by the French people could not develop. Consequently, an adaptation process has evolved: the power of a higher-ranking person is generally accepted and not challenged. In business life, people normally follow the instructions of a superior readily.

In contrast, the German federal system has a strong "[...] tradition of democratic decision-making [...]" (Scarborough, 1998, p. 215); equality between humans dates back to the Germanic *Gemeinschaftskultur*. Pateau, 1999

The high authority of French superiors as well as the supervision required by the employees resulted in an appreciation of the role of the French managers: "Der Erfolg einer Tochtergesellschaft steht und fällt mit ihrem Chef"[17] (Herterich, 2000, p. 28). French superiors have to be respected for their personality as well as for their professional competence. Furthermore, their strong ability to lead and control are indispensable for the efficiency of their team. Breuer & de Bartha, 2002

Fig. 9: Need a strong management. "This feels good."

Of course, this does not mean that these qualities are not important for German managers as well. The major difference however is, that in Germany managers are highly valued for their professional competence and their ability to coordinate. Their ability to lead is not as essential because even if a manager is lacking leadership skills, a team consisting of Germans will always be able to make decisions and work efficiently (Breuer & de Bartha, 2002). Moreover, an autocratic management style, which can often be found in French companies, would not be appropriate in Germany, since it is a *Small Power Distance* culture (see 3.1.1; Scarborough, 1998). In addition, German employees prefer a consensus-oriented decision-making style, which will be clarified in the following part.

5.2.1.2 Decision-making Style

There are various ways to come to a decision. German employees and superiors, who are part of a *collectivist* society (see 3.1.2), prefer a consensus-oriented decision-making style, whereas in French companies, a more dissent-oriented procedure is being applied.

In Germany, the first step is to present an idea in terms of a concept, which includes the main features of the idea as well as precise suggestions for action. This concept is dealt and discussed in detail by specialists; then a further specification of the concept is provided. On this basis, an agreement or a compromise is made which is to be presented to the boss afterwards. Generally, the German manager relies on his experts and therefore only checks certain key data. The function of the boss in this process is to coordinate and bring together the right people, who are able to reach an agreement; he only intervenes in case of a disaccord. Upon approval, the decision is accepted and accomplished without control. The employees do not further discuss it,

---

[17] *Suggested translation by the author:* "The success of an affiliate is totally dependant on its boss."

since they were able to speak out during the decision procedure (Breuer, & de Bartha, 2002). Although the German decision process is often criticised as being slow and inflexible, Scarborough (1998) explains its advantage: "Collectivism slows down the decision-making process but makes implementation easier and faster." (p. 263).

In France, "decision making is strictly top-down" (cited in Scarborough, 1998, p. 209). As the superiors know that people of *individualistic* societies (see 3.1.2) avoid processes, they usually decide on important issues alone. However, the key people are generally consulted beforehand; decisions of task groups are only considered as suggestions. Since the employees are usually not involved in the decision process, criticism is frequently expressed *after* a decision has been made. Breuer & de Bartha, 2002

The reasons for the varying decision-making styles of French and Germans can be traced back to historical developments. Since its creation in 1815, several attempts of Germany to unify the *Deutscher Bund* have been without success. The split-up of the federal states throughout history have encouraged give-and-take as well as cooperation among the population; therefore only minor hierarchical tendencies have evolved. In addition, consensus-oriented decision processes, which were indispensable to overcome regional differences, have developed. In contrast, French people have learned to accept top-down decisions due to the prevalent centralised power, as explained in the last chapter.

Power and control exert an important influence on business negotiations of French business people. The next chapter will focus on the 'power-thinking' of the French in contrast to the 'money-thinking' of the Germans.

5.2.1.3 Power vs. Money

French people think in terms of power. Just as the Germans, who love to talk about money, the French like to chat about power. Whereas too much force is considered negative in Germany, French people love to talk about this topic in bistros or even at family dinners.

Influential French people fear nothing more than loosing power and influence. Consequently, politicians and managers make every effort not to let foreign supervision take over traditional French companies. 'Laying of the foundation stone' for future power is already made during education. A small elitist ruling class, having attended one of the *Grandes Écoles*, occupies leading positions.

The striving for power can be noticed especially in business conversations. Since the French seek power and control, they expect a similar strategy from their counterparts. The French businessman tries to keep *la maîtrise*, the control, during a business meeting and dislikes 50/50 joint ventures as well as unequal cooperations. Breuer & de Bartha, 2002

This striving for power traces back to the monarchic society of Versailles in the 18th century. In those days, people did not work, but lived on their wealth. Power, prestige and social relations were the most important qualities in France at that time. Similar but more moderate values have developed at German courts. The repercussions can still be noticed today: French conversations are focused on an overriding desire to exercise control and to change the other person's opinion according to one's own wishes. The goal of such a conversation is to favour relations and to gain prestige and power. This behaviour is contrary to the German procedure, which is based on an issue focused, methodical, step-to-step procedure leading to agreement. Pateau, 1999

As already mentioned, money is an important core value for Germans. It enables them to buy things, which represent their social status. Germans try to stand out from the crowd through these material values; cars are a popular status symbol. Although Germans like to spend money, a clever handling is an important appraisal criterion in society. Due to historical reasons, wasting money, as well as bragging about wealth is regarded as disgrace. In addition, Germans love to highlight what a clever and reasonable bargain they have made. Mentioning of the price shows that the purchase was reasonable and efficient. Breuer & de Bartha, 2002

5.2.2 Differing Attitudes to Work

Working life in Germany often appears serious and cold, whereas in France people are always open for a chat with colleagues and prefer casual contacts. This attitude originates from the difference in German and French priorities. While Germans tend to focus on the actual task, French attach great importance to relationships. This contrast as well as the different attitudes concerning work performance will be subject of the next chapter. Since the core values influencing the French and German work attitudes differ considerably, it is obvious that different ways of motivating employees need to be applied. Therefore, the keys to motivate German and French employees will be the focal point in the last part of this chapter.

5.2.2.1 Task-Orientation vs. People-Orientation

Cultures can be divided into *task* and *people-orientated* societies, or according to Scarborough (1998) into: "doing" or "being" societies (p. 269). France belongs to the people-oriented cultures, whereas Germany is a task-oriented culture. Task and people-orientation are closely connected with the High and Low Context of Hall's dimensions (see 3.2.1). A strong relationship to a colleague encourages an indirect communication style. For fear of hurting the counterpart, a more diplomatic approach is employed and many things remain unsaid. In contrast, a more direct form of communication can be used if there is only a loose relationship between two colleagues. Disagreeable situations are therefore not feared and problems can be dealt with more thoroughly.

The difference in the communication style between Germans and French is based on their attitude towards relationships at work. French are more polite than Germans since they have a higher respect for their counterpart. In addition, they consider networking very important. Implicit communication as well as jokes and puns are not infrequent in French meetings. This dates back to the centralistic history of France, where, due to the minor regional differences, French people were not obliged to

Fig. 10: Meeting between Germans and French

express themselves explicitly; instead, they developed a more implicit, indirect, and quicker way of communication, which is often difficult to be followed by members of other cultures. In contrast, the explicit communication of the Germans is a product of high diversification concerning economy, regions, politics and religion. In order to be able to communicate with varying partners, a precise and clear way of expression was necessary. In France, a high level of context developed throughout its centralised development. Pateau, 1999

A collision of 'doing' and 'being' cultures, like France and Germany, may be the cause of severe misunderstandings. Germans should not think of the French as being lazy, but recognize that they have different priorities. They prefer relationships and family to business issues (Scarborough, 1998), whereas Germans are deal-oriented and focus on results (Lewis, 1999). Here, it can be referred to Hofstede's theory of Masculinity and Femininity (see 3.1.3); in which the French are described as being feminine. In addition, Germans working in France often notice the lack of communication in

German businesses and gradually appreciate the French way of staying in the office late for a chat with colleagues.

Furthermore, people-orientation may also be expressed by greeting or addressing someone. During an interview conducted for this thesis, a German manager, currently working in France, mentioned that he had observed his French boss greeting all his employees with a handshake *every morning*! This gesture illustrates the focus on relationship and the support of communication.

In addition, there is no common rule for addressing people; this depends on the corporate culture. Generally, all forms are possible: "vous" combined with the *surname*, "vous" combined with the *first name,* "tu" combined with the *surname* or "vous" combined with the *first name*. Recently, the form of "vous" in combination with the first name has been implemented, since the "vous" demonstrates respect and the *first name* allows closeness. In Germany, even after having worked together for several years, the formal "Sie" in combination with the surname, is used frequently; French colleagues find this rather surprising. Breuer & de Bartha, 2002

5.2.2.2 Functionality vs. Perfection

"Deutsche machen alles so gut wie möglich, Franzosen so gut wie nötig!"[18] (Breuer & de Bartha, 2002, p. 183); this quote illustrates another differing working attitude of the two cultures. Germans often admire the French ability to take time to live, which is based on the core value of *functionality;* in contrast, Germans are known for their striving for *perfection*.

French people are satisfied with a result as long as it serves its purpose; they see no necessity for absolute perfection and prefer to use the saved time to live or work out new ideas. This time saving aspect may also constitute a competitive advantage as far as production is concerned. E.g. the TGV does not have the same luxury and technology standards as its German counterpart, the ICE. Nevertheless the French train version represents a very fast and serviceable means of transportation.

In contrast, Germans are constantly aiming for perfection, whether regulations for products or tasks at work are concerned. The German perfection in project planning often results in a delay of the product launch. In addition, changes are difficult to

---

[18] *Suggested translation by the author:* "Germans do everything as well as possible, French as well as necessary."

realise after the approval of a product concept, since it is expected that the persons in charge have sufficiently checked every possible aspect concerning its operability. The German approach, to plan everything in detail, provides security and reliability; this can be traced back to the strong Uncertainty Avoidance of the Germans (see 3.1.4). Having in mind the task-orientation of the Germans, described in the last chapter, one can better understand their exactness in design, which creates confidence.

If we compare the German perfectionism with the French preference for functionality, it can be observed that French people try to achieve 80% functionality in their projects or products. Since they are constantly striving for innovation, they are more likely to see the *future potential*. Germans, on the other hand, focus on the remaining 20%, i.e. the details that make a project or a product perfect. Accordingly, the French tend to see the *risk potential*. Breuer & de Bartha, 2002

These attitudes may cause severe problems in a French-German project. The French, having only a very general concept (Breuer & de Bartha, 2002), will be faced with a lot of detailed questions about the project from their German colleagues. This will have a negative effect on the creativity of the French, which will be discussed in the next part.

5.2.2.3 Innovation vs. Conservatism

French are constantly looking for admiration and try to achieve functionality with a minimum effort. They do not like detailed planning, but prefer to have a general idea of a project (*globalement exact*). Therefore, creativity is not affected by details and can be used intuitively as a daily work technique, unlike in Germany, where extra facilitation techniques have been invented. This 'innovative thinking' is portrayed in many French products, which have dominated the market prominence for several years. A recent example is the fine particle filter, which has been part of the standard equipment of French Peugeot and Citroen cars since 2000 (Greenpeace Gruppe Aachen, 08/05) and is now in heavy demand as an update for German cars. However, since French employees are thinking of a new product as soon as the old one has been completed, they might run the risk of loosing sight of the *final* product by not adapting it to the changing market conditions. Breuer & de Bartha, 2002

In German companies, general ideas do not win recognition and therefore will be confronted with questions concerning their effectiveness as well as their reliability. The origin of this lies in the German core value of perfectionism. The Strong

Uncertainty Avoidance (see 3.1.4) of Germans, inhibits their interest in new applications and explains the "[...] search for familiar solutions rather than innovative ones" (Scarborough, 1998, p. 263). This is also the reason why products are often not bought for their brilliancy, but rather for their quality and reliability. Standards, which are permanently controlled, and in case of a failure the responsible person is brought to book.

Of course, this does not mean that Germans are not creative at all, but obviously their creativity is less dominant and often restricted. Breuer and de Bartha (2002) argue that the creativity of Germans is expressed in a different way. Their innovations are *improvements* of products, which can be traced back to their 'perfectionist thinking'. In contrast, since French love the challenge of global inventions, their innovations often are a real breakthrough.

In addition, difficulties arise frequently in the collaboration of these two cultures because French people often do not stick to a strategy, whereas Germans attach great importance to reliability and implementation. Since change and flexibility are motivation factors for French, they consider the decision process of the Germans as slow and inflexible. Breuer & de Bartha, 2002

5.2.2.4 Motivation – The Key for a Successful Cooperation

Motivation can be described as a key to induce somebody to act. It is either based on hope for a success or the avoidance of risks/an unpleasant situation. This chapter will mainly deal with the motivation factors of French people.

The generally known motivation techniques, like incentives or bonuses, imply that employees do not have sufficient motivation and result in the paradox that the employees only perform their required duties. Therefore, this chapter will address the 'non-financial' motivation techniques.

First of all, winning the sympathy of French employees is the most convenient way of motivating them; a good relationship with a French employee is an essential part of business life. In addition, French have a high capacity for enthusiasm; therefore the key for an efficient collaboration is to involve and not to restrain emotions. The more one is able to inspire the French partner for a certain idea, the more surprising and satisfying the results will be. Germans perform their daily work with enthusiasm,

French people, on the other hand, "[…] wollen Berge versetzen, mehr als das Ziel oder gar Unmögliches erreichen!"[19] (Breuer & de Bartha, 2002, p. 154). Consequently, French employees will achieve amazing results if they are motivated.

In addition, collectivist-cultures like Germany, attach great importance to teamwork, whereas French are more focused on their individual performance. Scarborough, 1998

But what happens if there is a lack of motivation? Unmotivated Germans will usually work less proactively, but they will at least perform their duties. Unmotivated French, however, will boycott or act contrary to their former promises. As this behaviour can be extremely harmful to a company, it is very important to keep French employees motivated; French managers therefore permanently identify unmotivated appointees.

Another key to motivate French employees is to address their core values. The most important ones have already been highlighted in the previous part, therefore a short listing will be sufficient: power, originality, challenge, admiration, liberty, functionality, change, and fun. In order to understand the core values of the other culture, one has to be able to develop empathy, i.e. to understand a culture in detail without judging it. Keeping this in mind, the next chapter aims at the reader's active performance to solve critical incidents between French and Germans. Breuer & de Bartha, 2002

---

[19] *Suggested translation by the author:* "[…] want to move mountains, reach more than the goal or even achieve the impossible!"

6 Empirical Review of the Culture Clash between French and Germans

In the following, cultural interactions will be analysed by applying the *Cultural Assimilator*, an intercultural learning concept, which will be illustrated in the first part of the chapter. These interactions, also called *critical incidents*, needed for the Cultural Assimilator, have been collected through an empirical research. After a description of the research method, the critical incidents will be described and evaluated.

6.1 The Concept of Cultural Assimilator

The Cultural Assimilator is a method for intercultural 'sensitization', which developed from a scientific study on communication at the University of Illinois/USA in 1966. The concept has also gained ground in Germany, where it was employed amongst others by Alexander Thomas, an author in the field of intercultural studies. The technique of the Cultural Assimilator is generally applied to the confrontation of two cultures or subcultures and describes interactions with the other culture leading to confusions, misinterpretations or even conflicts. Ohlemacher, 2004

In practice, the reader is confronted with similar situations and requested to choose between four possible suggestions for interpretation, but only one of them is correct. At this stage, the reader has to apply his knowledge gained from the theoretical part as well as his intercultural experience and associate it with the situation described in the question. After having decided on one of the answers, he is able to verify the accuracy of his choice by reading the explanations given in the following part.

The Cultural Assimilator provides a fast, inexpensive and relatively easy learning method; it helps to become familiar with and understand certain behaviour patterns of the other culture. Several studies relating to the concept of the Cultural Assimilator proved that by using this method, cultural awareness is created and social competence is increased (Ohlemacher, 2004). Besides, its application results in more sensibility when interacting with persons from the other culture and in some cases to an improved personal competence of the participants. They felt up to intercultural situations much better; anguishes and uncertainties were reduced (Albert, 1983).

In general, the Cultural Assimilator is a reliable and successful method of intercultural learning with diverse applications in role-plays, workshops or simulations.

6.1.1 Research Method

The interactions, also called *critical incidents*, have been gathered by means of interviews with various French and Germans, experienced in working life with the other culture. After a description of the sample, the applied research design and the method of collecting information will be explained in detail.

6.1.1.1 Description of Sample

The French and Germans interviewed for this study have one thing in common: contact to the respective culture. Among them were students and interns, as well as elder men and women who were able to acquire a lot of work experience with their foreign counterparts. The population sample consisted of a total of 21 people: 14 Germans and 7 French. The gender was distributed as follows: 12 male and 9 female. The age groups were between 22 and 66, the average age being 35.6. The median age was 35.6 and the mode 22. 15 individuals of the 21 sampled were 40 years old or younger.

The following chapter will first focus on the research design chosen, secondly on the interview method and finally on the resulting limitations.

6.1.1.2 Research Design

There are two types of researches mainly used in social sciences: *qualitative* and *quantitative*. Both types are part of the empirical social research, i.e. theoretical assumptions are verified in practice. The qualitative method is exploratory, whereas the quantitative is descriptive and causal/experimental. The difference between these two types of researches mainly consists of their basic items, structure and status of hypotheses as well as the implementation method. The quantitative research (often conducted by means of multiple choice questionnaires) is the numerical representation of observations for the purpose of verifying, describing and explaining a pre-defined theory. Due to this fact, the observations are restricted to subject areas. They are checked based on the assumption: social reality is regarded by all people in the same objective way. Since the reality is strongly limited by the previously determined data, quantitative research implies the danger of quantification and standardisation; the researcher modifies, influences, narrows and even provokes the results with his instrument.

This should be avoided when conducting a *qualitative research*, which is centred on subjective observations and aims at discovering underlying meanings and patterns of relationships within the naturally occurring context. This type of research is based on the assumption that people do not behave according to strict rules and norms, but constantly evaluate social situations. The structure of the qualitative research is neither intended to develop statistically valid samples nor does it apply standardised methods or predefined observation schemes. The research method consists of participant observation, interview, and document or artefact analysis (Wikipedia, 07/05); the sample of persons, as well as the situation of inquiry is chosen according to the research topic. The 'rule of thumb' to differentiate between the two research types is that quantitative research is a method of *verifying* hypotheses, whereas qualitative research is a method of *forming* hypotheses. Atteslander, 1995

In conjunction with the technique of the Cultural Assimilator, it is indispensable to conduct a qualitative research due to the fact that it allows analysing complex processes and their development (Heinze, 2001).

6.1.1.3 Method of Collecting Information

In order to collect the required information, individual depth interviews were conducted because an unstructured interview based on a questionnaire with open questions (see appendix) seemed to be especially appropriate. Most of the interviews were conducted face-to-face (14). Due to longer distances, particularly in case of French interviewees, some interviews were carried out by telephone (2); other questionnaires were received via email (5).

The intention when meeting the interviewee personally was to create a comfortable atmosphere. On this account, the interview was held in the respondent's mother tongue. After a self-introducing, the interviewer gave a short outline of the study and explained the objective of the interview. If the respondent agreed, the interview was audio taped and transcribed afterwards. In order to ease the flow of words and build up confidence, short and simple questions were asked initially. After having inquired about the length of stay in the other country, the first impression of the foreign culture and how the interviewee got in contact with the local people, the further questions were directed at raising the awareness of differences between the French and German culture (see appendix A: questionnaire interviewees). The central part of the interview constituted asking for an intercultural experience, which seemed unusual to the respondent or which he/she could not understand at first (=*critical incident*). If necessary, the term *critical incident* was briefly explained. The interview was terminated after 30-60 minutes with a final question asking about how the interviewee had been prepared by his/her company and if this kind of preparation was regarded as necessary.

6.1.1.4 Limitations

Although all interviewees had been in intensive contact with the other culture, the question on the *critical incident* caused many interviewees to reflect about it for a long time. Frequently, they were not able to recall an experienced situation. Most of the respondents only referred to the general behaviour of the other culture without being able to describe a specific situation. Alexander Thomas explains this phenomenon as follows: "Wenn man Gespräche mit Menschen führt, die über langjährige eigene Erfahrungen in der Kommunikation mit Menschen einer spezifischen Fremdkultur verfügen, und wenn man sie im Rahmen teilstrukturierter Interviews systematisch über ihre Beobachtungen erwartungswidrigen Verhaltens fragt, stellt man fest, dass sie dazu neigen, ihre Beobachtungen auf einem relativ hohen Abstraktionsniveau in Form typischer und charakteristischer allgemeiner Merkmale und Eigenschaften zu kategorisieren."[20] (Thomas, 2003, p. 103). He further states that these people often have difficulties in describing specific situations as well as their emotions, expectations and thoughts. Everyday communication and interaction with the other culture is obviously recalled and communicated as the summed-up knowledge of a typical cultural behaviour. "Es bedarf einer sorgfältigen Interviewführung, um verhaltensnah interkulturelle Interaktionssituationen geschildert zu bekommen"[21] (Thomas, 2003, p. 103). On the basis of this experience and knowledge, the respondents of further interviews were informed beforehand about the term *critical incident* and that during the interview they would be asked to describe a specific experienced situation; some of these incidents will be specified in the following sections.

---

[20] *Suggested translation by the author:* "When talking to people, who have a long experience in communicationg with people of a specific foreign culture, and if they are systematically asked, in the course of partly structured interviews, if they had observed any unusual behaviour, it can be noticed that they tend to categorise their observations on a relatively high abstraction level; usually in the form of typical and characteristic features and qualities."

[21] *Suggested translation by the author:* "In order to have interviewees describe true behaviour of intercultural interactions, the interview has to be conducted thoroughly."

6.2 Critical Incidents

Does French leadership irritate you? Why do French people not adhere to deadlines? Do business lunches have to be longer than absolutely necessary? Why do French constantly argue during meetings and are insufficiently prepared?

A number of critical incidents are presented below. By choosing one of the four answers given, the reader is supposed to see the contact with the other culture from a process perspective. Then, basic knowledge about each cultural interaction, which will be useful for intercultural interactions in the future, will be imparted. Thus, the reader is to be sensitised for such processes enabling him to successfully analyse similar situations. With the acquired understanding for the other culture, the above-mentioned questions can be answered without difficulty.

6.2.1 Student-Teacher Relationship

A German girl (22), who studied in France for 3 ½ years and only recently gained an insight into working life, mentioned the difficulties she had experienced while attending university in France. Most of the time, she had been the only one to participate in lectures. Furthermore, she stated that she had rarely noticed conversations between professors and students. Despite the French students' enthusiasm for the subject matter, they refrained from asking questions, nor did they take an active part in class discussions. Obviously, they were satisfied with taking notes which conveyed the impression that the theoretical contents were 'soaked up like a sponge'. Lecturers were never criticised face-to-face, but only among students, if at all. The interviewee remarked in addition that her fellow students gave her weird looks when she argued with a professor during the lecture or when she talked to him/her outside class. Some of them had even told her that they did not understand her attitude towards professors.

What is the reason for the low participation of the French students in class and their reserved behaviour towards teachers/professors outside class?

6.2.1.1 Possible Solutions

A. French students are less interested in theoretical knowledge as well as in personal contact with their professors.

B. French students consider personal talks with professors as well as criticising them as impolite.
C. French students are eager to learn and therefore want to take notes of every word their professor says. That leaves them little time to ask questions, participate in class or have a private talk with lecturers.
D. French students are afraid of asking silly questions in front of their fellow students. They are also too shy to talk to their professors outside class.

6.2.1.2 Explanation

The following critical incident came up several times during the interviews conducted with German students who studied in France. Although this situation might not be of particular relevance to business at first glance, it has repercussions on the working environment, which will be shown below.

Solution B is correct. The incident clearly represents the clash between a *Large* and a *Small Power Distance* nation. Large Power Distance countries, like France (see 3.1.1), are characterised by a strong "parent-child […]", and consequently, a "teacher-student inequality" (Hofstede, 1997, p. 32). Already in grade school – children are expected to know what the teachers tell them; they are neither taught to participate nor to develop individually. Children and students treat their teachers with respect. The education is teacher-centred; his guidelines are to be followed. Students are supposed to speak up only in case their teachers ask them to do so. In addition, teachers are not criticised in public and, even outside school, students have respect for their instructors. Due to a rather personalised education style, the quality of learning depends to a large extent on the capability of the teachers. Small power distance countries, like Germany, support equality between parents and children and therefore teachers treat their students as equals and vice versa. German students are encouraged to be proactive in class and ask questions. The education in Germany is more student-centred, motivating the students to find their own way of learning. Disagreement with and criticism of teachers is expressed face-to-face; students are not particularly respectful towards their teachers outside school. Since the education system in Small Power Distance countries is based on the students' independence, the quality of the lessons is dependant on the students´ initiative. Hofstede, 1997
Human behaviour is largely determined by knowledge acquired during childhood. Keeping in mind the example of French children, who are taught to attach great

importance to the respect of elders and superiors, the consequences for working life becomes apparent as shown in chapter 5.2.1.1, where the distinct authority of French managers is explained.

In addition, Breuer and de Bartha (2002) state "Deutsche sagen direkt heraus was sie denken"[22] (p. 296). This statement was approved by a French woman (42), working in a German-French corporation located in France, who was interviewed for this thesis: "La traitment de la critique est plus directe en Allemagne que chez nous. Quand on a un problème avec un Allemand, il appelle et dit qu´il a un problème avec toi pour telle et telle raison. En France, on va essayer de faire comprendre qu'on a un problème sans oser le dire si ouvertement."[23] Thus, the high-context French prefer harmony and do not express themselves as direct as Germans (see 3.2.1; 5.2.2.1).

With this in mind, one can understand better, why French students/people accept authority and have respect for it, as described in the incident above. As a consequence, they consider asking questions, expressing disagreement in the presence of the teacher/professor as well as personal talks with the instructor as impolite and disrespectful. Germans, in contrast, regard questioning elders and superiors as normal, many teachers and professors even appreciate students´ commitment, participation and criticism.

Solution A is not correct because it cannot be generalised that French students do not like to study. Moreover, personal contacts with professors are not the result of a lack of interest, but are simply not common.

Solution C is not correct. Like in solution A, the thirst for knowledge cannot be generalised because there are busy as well as relaxed students.

Solution D is not correct, since, due to a high degree of individualism, most French people are not afraid of giving their opinion; on the contrary, they are very proud of it.

---

[22] *Suggested translation by the author:* "Germans express what they think in a direct way."

[23] *Suggested translation by the author:* "Criticism is expressed more directly in Germany than in our country. If you are having problems with a German, he will call you and let you know that a problem has arisen between you and him for such and such a reason. In France, if people have a problem, they will try to insinuate the issue without expressing it directly."

6.2.2 An Unanswered Email

A German product manager, employed at OSRAM GmbH, Munich, who grew up close to the French boarder, confirmed several times during the interview that he got along very well with the French and their way of life. He stated that he never had experienced any difficulties with the French culture. In the course of the conversation, he explained that it was easier to collaborate with French people if a personal relationship had already been established. Asked whether he sometimes had difficulties in finding the right contact person or receiving answers from French colleagues, he answered that he had been frustrated recently, because he had not received an answer to an email he had sent out to two French colleagues. Even after having sent an email reminder, there was no reaction even though he had known the two French colleagues personally. The German product manager stated further that he was finally able to solve the problem by talking to the boss of his colleagues.

Why did the German product manager not receive an answer to his email even after following up?

6.2.2.1 Possible Solutions

A. French people prefer phone calls to emails and are not accustomed to answer without prior consultation of their superior.
B. Since French people are very individualistic, they do not like to receive emails, which are addressed to two persons at the same time.
C. Due to historical events, French people distrust Germans innately.
D. French have an aversion to other languages; consequently they take more time to answer emails not written in French.

6.2.2.2 Explanation

Solution A is correct. French people prefer verbal communication, and, as a consequence, they dislike receiving too many written briefings. In contrast, Germans are known for their explicitness in expression accompanied by the most important items in writing (Breuer & de Bartha, 2002). In addition, they usually attach the same importance to phone calls and emails. Since French people prefer verbal information, calling a French colleague is much more efficient than writing an email or a fax. The reason for this is probably the people-orientation of the French compared to the task-orientation of the Germans (see 5.2.2.1). Since countries with a strong people-orientation, attach great importance to personal relationships, they favour phone calls or meetings more than emails because personal information can be passed on more easily. The task-oriented Germans often get annoyed with the French talking about personal things and get frustrated when their French colleagues do not come straight to the point.

In addition, one of the most frequent problems for Germans, who directly collaborate with French, is the fact that it is very difficult to find the right contact person being endued with technical knowledge as well as with power of decision. As it can be read in chapter 5.2.1.2, it occurs very often in France that the boss decides alone. This means that the employee spends a lot of time consulting the superior about the matter. German employees, who are quite independent in their decisions, are often surprised by the absence of the delegation of power in French companies (Pateau, 1999).

The reason why the above-mentioned incident happened is, first of all, the different communication styles of French and Germans, and secondly, the difficulty in addressing the right contact person who is authorised to release information.

Solution B is not correct. Although French, who want to distance themselves from 'normal' people can be characterised as individualistic (see 3.1.2), it is very unlikely that they will be offended by an email with two addressees.

Solution C is not correct. Historical events will often be remembered for a long time and may evoke resentment towards the other nation. However, since Osram is an international company, it is rather improbable that this will lead to a refusal of cooperation with German employees.

Solution D is not correct. Although it is true that French people prefer conversations (written or verbal) in their native language (see 4.2.2), there is no evidence from the incident that the email was written in a language other than French. Furthermore, the fact that OSRAM is an international company reduces the probability that emails in another language will be answered later than emails in native language.

6.2.3 Business Negotiation

A German manager, working at Osram GmbH in Munich, had several business contacts with his French colleagues and business partners. Most of the time, he had no problems in dealing with the other culture, but in the course of the conducted interview, he mentioned one incident where he could not understand the reaction of his French partner: For the final negotiations with a French company about a product cooperation, the German manager arranged a meeting with the responsible French counterpart. During the conversation, the German manager realised that he outclassed his French partner from a technical point of view. The German manager intended to refer to the product, as a *French-German cooperation*, but the French colleague did not agree - he insisted on calling the product a *pure French* one. The German manager had the impression that his French partner wanted to demonstrate power and even after several attempts he did not succeed in changing the mind of his counterpart. Finally they were able to solve the problem by eating out together the same evening. In the course of the meal, the French found out that his German partner had some knowledge of French cuisine; they even realised that they preferred the same type of wine.

Why was the French businessman not willing to cooperate with his German counterpart until they had dinner together?

6.2.3.1 Possible Solutions

A. In France, it is not common to decide on business issues before having lunch or dinner together; visitors are expected to adhere to this 'rule'.
B. French people have a very distinct national pride; therefore French managers try to do everything to refer to a good product as being of 'French origin'.
C. Power and control are very important to French people. Consequently, by agreeing to call the product a 'German-French cooperation', the French businessman thinks that he has lost influence and power.
D. The atmosphere during the meeting was too formal for the French businessman because French people prefer a relaxed atmosphere for negotiations.

6.2.3.2 Explanation

Solution C is correct. In order to understand the background of this incident, one has to keep in mind that French people think in terms of power. Their striving for power and control affects every business conversation and leads to a general refusal of 50/50 joint ventures or co operations (see 5.2.1.3).

Referring to the incident, it is now easier to understand why the French businessman was constantly aiming at taking the lead during the negotiation. He was afraid of loosing power to his German counterpart who seemed to be technically superior in the first place. Since the German manager was not aware of the strategy of his French partner, who aimed at maximizing his influence and power on the project, he could not understand the reaction of his French partner.

Keeping this in mind, the question arises why the French businessman *did* finally give in during their dinner. The answer is that the atmosphere during the meal facilitated a relaxed conversation and contributed to an improved relationship of the two businessmen. The French felt respected and acknowledged by his German partner and realised that the German was not 'playing a game' to gain power. Consequently, the French changed his mind with respect to the issue of their business negotiation.

Solution A can also be considered as correct. Since French want to detect the counterpart's weaknesses, strengths and intentions, they usually have lunch or dinner with their partner *before* signing a contract (Breuer & de Bartha, 2002). Although this solution may be regarded as true, the refusal of the French businessman originated from the French 'power' and 'strategy-thinking', which has been explained previously.

Solution B is not correct. It is true that French people have a very distinct national pride (see 4.2.2). Although this attitude might have had an influence on the behaviour of the French businessman, it was not the main reason for the misunderstanding (see solution C).

Solution D is not correct. It cannot be generalised that French people need a relaxed atmosphere to make a decision. As it can be stated in the explanation solution C, the change of atmosphere probably contributed to solve the problem, but it was not the only reason for the persistency of the French businessman.

6.2.4 Time Management

Another German product manager, employed at the marketing department of OSRAM GmbH, asked one of his French colleagues, whom he had known personally, to write an article about a successful project. This article was to be released in the quarterly published sales bulletin of the marketing department. The deadline for the article was set for December 15, but despite several reminders, the German manager did not receive the article until December 23.

Why did the French colleague not meet the deadline for the article?

6.2.4.1 Possible Solutions

A. French people have a different time perception; deadlines do not have the same priority as in Germany.
B. In December, people in France are rather focused on buying presents for Christmas – work life is of secondary importance; foreigners are expected to accept this.
C. Due to a family reunion, the French colleague was not able to meet the deadline.
D. The French colleague did not deliver the article in due time, since he is unorganised like most French.

6.2.4.2 Explanation

Solution A is correct. This incident is a classic example of cultural differences between Germans and French, which equals the stereotype of the unpunctual French. The reason for this incident is the different time perception between the two cultures. Breuer & de Bartha, 2002

In his book "Understanding Cultural Differences", Hall explains that Germans are known for their punctuality (see 3.2.3). For them, people who adhere to deadlines are considered reliable; tardy colleagues are regarded as not organized. In contrast, French people, due to their high level of flexibility, do not like to keep to precise dates. They take it for granted that others do not meet deadlines (Breuer & de Bartha, 2002) and, in addition, they attach great importance to relationships (see 5.2.2.1) and like to be *challenged* (see 5.2.2.4).

Having gained this knowledge, it becomes apparent, why the French manager did not write the requested article in time. First of all, since he belongs to a relationship-oriented culture, he did not give the article a top priority. In addition, he did not consider the duty to be a very challenging one, which resulted in a weak motivation. Furthermore, he would have expected a delay of the deadline because of the personal relationship to his German partner (Breuer & de Bartha, 2002). Finally, the German manager made a 'mistake' by writing an *email* reminder to his French colleague. Since relationship-oriented cultures, like France, prefer phone calls to written communication (see 6.2.3.2), the French manager may have felt defensive by receiving *only* an email.

Solution B is wrong. Although the Christmas season may be a rather hectic time for many cultures, this was certainly not the main reason for the French manager to refrain from writing the article in time (see solution A).

Solution C is not correct. Due to the fact that French attach great importance to family and relationships, a family reunion might have been a possible reason for the French manager not to deliver the article in time. However, a family reunion is normally not a matter of a few weeks and therefore could not have been the cause for the delay.

Solution D is wrong. Although it is true that French people tend to be less organised than Germans, this is not the adequate solution. Despite their unorganized behaviour (which is of course not true for all French), French people are often capable of fulfilling tasks in a better way than their German colleagues.

6.2.5 An Act of Friendship

A French manager had been working at the German headquarter of OSRAM GmbH for several years. At the very beginning of his employment in Germany, one of his German female colleagues asked him to do her a favour: to buy her a certain perfume on his next visit to France. When, on his return, the French manager gave her the perfume in the office, the German woman asked what she owed him besides the purchase price. The French manager answered intuitionally: "*deux bises*"[24]. When she refused with a frightened look, he realized that he had made a mistake.

Why did the German woman react like this?

6.2.5.1 Possible Solutions

A. The German woman was afraid that someone could watch her and the French manager exchanging kisses in the office.
B. Since Germans are not used to such closeness and affection, the German woman refused because she thought that the French manager had only brought the perfume along because he had a 'deeper intention'.
C. Since the German woman did not speak French well, she understood that she owed him two times the purchase price.

---

[24] *Suggested translation by the author:* "two kisses"

D. She was embarrassed because the French manager had given her the perfume in the office; in Germany, it is not customary to exchange private things at work.

6.2.5.2 Explanation

Solution B is right. According to Hall, Germans need a relatively large personal space, compared to other cultures (see 3.2.2). This originates from their task-orientation (see 5.2.2.1). Closeness, hugs and kisses are only allowed among good friends; strangers and business colleagues are expected to keep a certain distance. If the Germans´ personal space is not respected, a cool reaction is very likely.

Going back to the incident, the reaction of the German women becomes understandable. When the French manager asked her for two kisses, she felt cornered and very uncomfortable because they had only a business relationship.

A similar incident was brought up in another interview with a 22-year-old girl, who had worked as a waitress in France. "Die typische Begrüßung – la bise – ist mir anfangs unangenehm gewesen. Ich habe mich recht schnell daran gewöhnt, doch bei einem Kollegen, habe ich mich nach einiger Zeit geweigert ihn auf diese Weise zu begrüßen, da ich ihn nicht sympathisch fand und das Gefühl hatte, als würde er dabei immer weiter Körperkontakt suchen. Ich war mir darüber klar, dass das ein offener Affront ihm gegenüber war, was sich auf unser Arbeitsverhältnis ausgewirkt hat, dennoch konnte ich nicht über meinen Schatten springen."[25]

Having understood the cause for the behaviour of the German woman, the question remains to be asked why the French manager had requested two kisses. In France, it is very common to kiss on every possible occasion. The general way of greeting somebody consists of two to four kisses on each cheek alternately (depending on the region). Hereby it does not matter if the person is a good friend or not. In business, the way of greeting may be handled differently depending on the corporate culture and the individual person. In addition, it is a general behaviour pattern to ask for two kisses in return of something; nobody in France will feel offended by this.

---

[25] *Suggested translation by the author:* "At first, the typical greeting – the kiss – was of some embarrassment to me. I got accustomed to it rather quickly, but after some time I refused to greet one of my colleagues in such a way because I disliked him. Furthermore, I had the feeling that in doing so he kept approaching me physically. Although, I was clear in my mind that he would be offended by this, and that this affected our working relationship, I could not bite the bullet."

After having understood the behaviour of both, the French manager and his German colleague, it becomes apparent that this incident represented a typical clash of the two cultures.

Solution A is not correct. Although this may be a possible explanation, it is not the right one (see solution B).

Solution C is wrong. There is evidence from the incident that the woman was not able to speak French and was not able to understand what her French colleague was saying. Therefore this solution cannot be considered as the right one.

Solution D is not correct. There is no general rule like the one mentioned. Although Germans like to separate between business and private life, especially younger generations have no problem in combining the two.

6.2.6 A Chaotic Meeting

A German woman, employed at MAN, took part in a meeting concerning the organisational structure of their joint venture with a French affiliate. Of course, her team, only consisting of Germans, had prepared a detailed concept on which they had been working on for the last four months. Throughout the presentation of the concept, the French were constantly asking questions and requesting changes without making *precise* suggestions. The Germans were upset and the meeting ended without concrete results.

Why had the meeting not been successful?

6.2.6.1 Possible Solutions

A. French people are never sufficiently prepared for meetings.
B. Due to their high level of individuality, French do not like to accept a concept without discussing it.
C. The French felt cornered by the detailed concept of their German colleagues; their intention was to discuss the topic first and not to come to a precise conclusion right away.
D. The Germans began to present their concept without allowing enough time for personal talks, which annoyed the French.

6.2.6.2 Explanation

Solution D is correct. Germans and French have a completely different perception of an efficient meeting. Germans, on the one hand, usually expect concrete results from a meeting; French, on the other hand, arrange meetings in order to discuss, for the purpose of exchanging ideas and brainstorming a topic.

An agenda therefore serves as a guideline for the French which does not have to be kept; this attitude may be a result of their high flexibility (see 5.2.2.3). If current issues have a higher priority than the original agenda of the French, they will be discussed right away; a target-performance comparison is considered unnecessary and exhausting. Breuer & de Bartha, 2002

In contrast, Germans want to reach a decision promptly and therefore consider a meeting without precise results inefficient. This attitude originates from the target-orientation (see 5.2.2.1) of the Germans. On the other hand, the detailed preparation of the concept results from their tendency to fulfil all duties perfectly (see 5.2.2.2).

Reflecting on the incident, one can better understand why the French had attended the meeting without being sufficiently prepared. Their objective was to favour an active exchange of thoughts. Another reason for the constant interruptions of the French employees could have been the missing emotion and challenge (see 5.2.2.3). In addition, the Germans were upset because they had a completely different expectation of the meeting: they wanted to come to a decision. Since this was not achieved, the Germans considered the outcome of the meeting as a waste of time.

Solution A is not correct. Although this statement is a frequent prejudice, it is not true. The preparation for a meeting of French may probably not be as detailed as the Germans´, but their flexibility and the exchange of ideas favour their creativity and often results in innovative ideas.

Solution B is wrong. While it is true that French are rather individualistic (see 3.1.2), this statement is generally unfounded.

Solution C is partly correct. French attach great importance to personal relationships which are essential for business (see 5.2.2.1). The immediate presentation by the Germans did not leave any time for small talk between the business partners. This could indeed have been a reason why the French did not cooperate. Nevertheless, it is more likely that the meeting had failed from the Germans´ point of view due to the different expectations of the two parties (see solution D).

6.3 Suggestions for a Better Cooperation with French People

The following hints are a result from the author's personal experience and will, in addition to the already provided information, back up this thesis.

Although, the different language may constitute a barrier, it can be overcome much easier than the prevailing stereotypes. However, it may be noted that, once a German is able to speak the French language, the approach to French people is a lot simpler.

Moreover, sympathy is extremely important in order to cooperate with French people: jokes, as well as common meals and talks about Germany or France will create a favourable atmosphere.

What should also be kept in mind is that French, in order accomplish good results, must be challenged and motivated by a task. In addition, one should allow them their independence in accomplishing a task, as they like to work according to *their* procedure.

For working in France, it is essential to forget the German values of efficiency. First of all, since French do not attach great importance to keeping with time schedules, one should try to get used to this behaviour pattern. Although the French attitude of completing tasks in the last minute may lead to insecurity and unnecessary time pressure from the German point of view, one can be sure that they will succeed.

Moreover, one should not become upset if French colleagues are late for appointments or meetings. Since they will hardly change their behaviour, it is better to set a liberal time frame for meetings. Besides, the additional time might as well be used for a chat with another colleague and therefore contribute to extend one's network.

In addition, it was mentioned in this thesis that Germans tend to fulfil their duties with a sense of perfectionism (see 5.2.2.2). French people will often not achieve these standards since their focus is set on the functionality of a task.

For most incidents and different behaviour styles, a simple method needs to be applied: The incident or different attitudes need to be discussed between all participants. Only an open approach will help to prevent misunderstandings and problems. Finally, it has to be kept in mind, that there is no use in criticising the other culture and the associated behaviour patterns. It has to be accepted, that there are other, unconventional, ways of accomplishing a task. *They are by no means bad, but only different.*

7 Conclusion

This thesis has shown how behaviour patterns of the German and French culture have developed from an interaction of history, geography, society and education. Cultural differences, their origin, and especially the repercussions on business life, have been described in theory and accompanied by practical examples. Hereby, an understanding for the cultural differences of the French has been established which was the aim of this thesis.

Recapping, it can be said that there have been many efforts to contribute to an improvement of the French-German relationship over the centuries. Nevertheless, it has to be kept in mind that town twinnings, student exchanges, mergers and intercultural trainings etc. will help to increase interaction and therefore more understanding of the other culture, but only if *respect* and *tolerance* will be applied.

Concerning business life, it has become apparent throughout this thesis that Germans and French have extremely opposed qualities.

These qualities were summed up in a survey of 200 German-French corporations, in which managers were asked to name the preferred qualities of the respective culture. A short extract of the result is as follows (Breuer & de Bartha, 2002, p. 90):

German managers prefer the following qualities of the French	French managers prefer the following qualities of the Germans
➢ flexibility ➢ creativity ➢ savoir-vivre ➢ spontaneity ➢ improvisation ➢ enthusiasm ➢ engagement	➢ reliability ➢ accuracy ➢ thoroughness ➢ punctuality ➢ pragmatism ➢ efficiency ➢ professionalism

Taking a closer look, it becomes evident, that the French qualities are mainly based on emotion, whereas the German attributes are based on reason and facts. Therefore, one must realize that the traits of the French and Germans represent an 'ideal complementary' and may be a perfect contribution to the performance of a team.

Both, German and French managers and employees, who are aware of this fact, will benefit from the cultural differences existing in their team / corporation using it as a competitive advantage in the changing market environment.

Bibliography

Books

Albert, R. (1983), *The Intercultural Sensitizer or Culture Assimilator: A Cognitive Approach*, in: Landis, D. and Brislin, R. (eds.), Handbook of Intercultural Training, Pergamon Press, New York, USA

Atteslander, P. (1995), *Methoden der empirischen Sozialforschung*, 8th edition, de Gruyter, Berlin, Germany

Barmeyer, C. (1996), *Interkulturelle Qualifikationen im deutsch-französischen Management kleiner und mittelständischer Unternehmen,* Röhrig Universitätsverlag St. Ingberg, Germany

Barmeyer, C. (1999), *Landeskundliche und interkulturelle Kompetenzen im deutsch-französischen Training. Das Beispiel grenzüberschreitender Handwerksbetriebe. –* In: Kulturunterschiede/ Hahn, H. (eds.), IKO-Verlag für interkulturelle Kommunikation, Frankfurt am Main, Germany

Berting, J. et al. (1995), *Stereotypes and Nations*, Drukarnia UJ, Cracow, Poland

Breuer, P. & de Bartha, P. (2002), *Deutsch-Französische Geschäftsbeziehungen erfolgreich managen,* Fachverlag Deutscher Wirtschaftsdienst GmbH & CO. KG, Köln, Germany

Chevènement, J-P. (1996), *France-Allemagne*, Parlons franc, Plon, Paris, France

Colard, D. (1999), *Le Partenariat Franco-Allemand – Du Traité de l'Elysée à la République de Berlin (1963-1999)*, Editor Gualino, Paris, France

Fischer, M. (1996), *Interkulturelle Herausforderungen im Frankreichgeschäft. Kulturanalyse und interkulturelles Management,* Gabler Verlag, Deutscher Universitäts-Verlag, Wiesbaden, Germany

Fischer, W. (1991), *Grundwissen Landeskunde – La France,* Ernst Klett Schulbuchverlag GmbH, Stuttgart, Germany

Der Fischer Weltalmanach – *Daten, Zahlen und Fakten* (2004)

Gibson, R. (1998), *International Communication in Business Theory and Practice*, Verlag Wissenschaft & Praxis, Berlin, Germany

Grosse, E. & Lüger H. (1994), *Understanding France in Comparison with Germany* (1987 first edition), European Academic Publishers, Bern/Suisse

Hahn, H. (1999), *Kulturunterschiede: interdisziplinäre Konzepte zu kollektiven Identitäten und. Mentalitäten.* IKO- Verlag für interkulturelle Kommunikation, Frankfurt am Main, Germany

Hall, E. (1990), *Understanding Cultural Differences*, Intercultural Press, Maine, USA

Hecht-El Minshawi, B. (2003), *Interkulturelle Kompetenz – For a better understanding*, Weinheim, Beltz Verlag, Basel/ Suisse, Berlin/ Germany

Heinze, T. (2001), *Qualitative Sozialforschung*, Oldenbourg Wissenschaftsverlag GmbH, München, Germany

Herterich, K. (1991), *Deutsch-französische Führungs- und Personalberatung*, Paris France

Herterich, K. (2000), *Management deutscher Unternehmen in Frankreich*, Deutsch-Französische Industrie- und Handelskammer, Paris, France

Hofstede, G. (1997), *Cultures and Organizations: Software of the mind*, First Edition 1991, McGraw-Hill, New York, USA

Lüsebrink, H-J. (2000), *Einführung in die Landeskunde Frankreichs*, J. B. Metzler Verlag, Stuttgart/Weimar, Germany

Pateau, J. (1999), *Die seltsame Alchimie in der Zusammenarbeit von Deutschen und Franzosen: Aus der Praxis des interkulturellen Managements*, Campus Verlag, New York, USA

Scarborough, J. (1998), *The origins of cultural differences and their impact on management*, Quorum Books, Westport, USA

Schäfer, H., Jung, R. & Seibel, F. (1994) in: *Vielfalt gestalten – Managing diversity*, IKO-Verlag für Interkulturelle Kommunikation, Frankfurt am Main, Germany

Stiftung Haus der Geschichte (1998), *Vis-à-vis: Deutschland und Frankreich,* DuMont Buchverlag, Köln, Germany

Thomas, A., Kinast, E. & Schroll-Machl, S. (2003), *Handbuch Interkulturelle Kommunikation und Kooperation, Band 1: Grundlagen und Praxisfelder*, Vandenhoeck & Rupprecht, Göttingen, Germany

Thomas, A., Kammhuber, S. & Schroll-Machl, S. (2003), *Handbuch Interkulturelle Kommunikation und Kooperation, Band 2: Länder, Kulturen und interkulturelle Berufstätigkeit*, Vandenhoeck & Rupprecht, Göttingen, Germany

Zimmermann, M. (1995), *Kultur : Culture, Zum Verhältnis zwischen Deutschen und Franzosen*, Institut für Kulturanthropologie und Europäische Ethnologie, Frankfurt am Main, Germany

Documents

Auswärtiges Amt, Rede von Bundesaußenminister Fischer vor dem Deutschen Bundestag zum 40. Jahrestag des Élysée-Vertrages, viewed 27 July 2005, <www.auswaertiges-amt.de/www/de/eu_politik/ausgabe_archiv?archiv_id=3953&type_id=3&bereich_id=4

DAAD (2003), *SOKRATES/ERASMUS – Studierendenmobilität aus deutscher Sicht 2001/2002*, Statistische Übersichten zur Realisierung

Dance, F. (1970), *The concept of communication*, Journal of Communication, 20, pp. 201-210

Deutsche Bundesregierung, *Common declaration on the occasion of the 40th anniversary of the Elysée Treaty between Chirac and Schröder* (2003), viewed 27 July 2005, <www.bundesregierung.de/emagazine_entw-,413.463558/Gemeinsame-Erklaerung-zum-40.-.htm>

Hart, W. B. (1997), *A Brief History of Intercultural Communication: A Paradigmatic Approach*, Paper presented at the Speech Communication Association Convention, San Diego, USA

McSweeney, B. (2002), *Hofstede's 'Model of National Cultural Differences and Consequences: A Triumph of Faith - A Failure of Analysis*, Human Relations', 55.1, 89-118, viewed 1 July 2005, <http://geert-hofstede.international-business-center.com/mcsweeney.shtml>

Picht, R. & Kolle, A., *Abschlussbericht des Teilprojekts: Auf dem Weg in die europäische Wissensgesellschaft. Perspektiven deutscher und französischer Bildungspolitik*, viewed 3 July 2005, <www.asko-europa-stiftung.de/zukunftswerkstatt/franz/veroeffentlichung.htm>

Websites

Auswärtiges Amt, viewed 15 February 2005,
<www.auswaertiges-amt.de>

Bundeszentrale für politische Bildung, viewed 19 August 2005,
<www.bpb.de/publikationen/JA9S1J,0,0,Deutschfranz%F6sische_Beziehungen.html>

Der Spiegel, viewed 20 March 2005,
<www.derspiegel.de>

Deutschland.de, Deutschland auf einen Blick, viewed 15 May 2005,
<www.deutschland.de>

DGAP, viewed 1 August 2005,
<www.dgap.org>

Eurocorps, viewed 19 August 2005,
<www.eurocorps.org>

Französische Botschaft, Frankreich – Info (12/2002), viewed 20 May 2005,
<www.botschaft-frankreich.de>

Greenpeace Gruppe Aachen, viewed 19 August 2005,
<http://gruppen.greenpeace.de/aachen/dieselruss.html>

Ohlemacher, A. (2004), Institut für interkulturelle Didaktik e.V. (IKUD),
viewed 1 August 2005, < www.ikud.de/iikdiaps1-93.htm>

Statistisches Bundesamt Deutschland, viewed 1 August 2005,
<www.destatis.de/indicators/d/arb210ad.htm>

The World Factbook, viewed 3 May 2005,
<www.cia.gov/cia/publications/factbook/index.html>

Tradeport, viewed 23 August 2005,
<www.tradeport.org/countries/france/01grw.html>

Wikipedia- the Free Encyclopedia, viewed 20 May 2005, <www.wikipedia.org>

<www.analytictech.com>, viewed 1 August 2005

<www.deutschland-und-frankreich.de>, viewed 1 August 2005

Journal Articles

Ecoute, *De la guerre et de la paix entre la France et l'Allemagne*, interview with Georges Valance, écoute 3/2000, p. 69

Pusch, M. & Hoopes, D. (1979), *Intercultural Communication Concepts and the Psychology of Intercultural Experience*. in Pusch, M. (Ed.) Multicultural Education: A Cross-Cultural Training Approach, Intercultural Press, Yarmouth, Maine, USA

Shackleton, Viv J. and Ali, Abbas H. (1990), *Work-related values of managers: a test of the Hofstede model*. Journal of Cross-Cultural Psychology, 21(1): p. 109-118

Sorrells K. (1998), *Gifts of Wisdom: An Interview with Dr. Edward T. Hall*, The Edge: The E-Journal of Intercultural Relations, Vol. 1(3), viewed 16 June 2005, <http://interculturalrelations.com/v1i3Summer1998/sum98sorrellshall.htm>

UNESCO, *UNESCO Universal Declaration on Cultural Diversity* (2002), viewed 15 May 2005, <www.unesco.org/education/imld_2002/unversal_decla.shtml>

Dissertations

Dahl, S (2004), *Intercultural Research: The Current State of Knowledge*, Middlesex University Business School Discussion Paper, viewed 4 June, 2005, <http://mubs.mdx.ac.uk/Research/Discussion_Papers/Marketing/dpap%20marketing%20no26.pdf>

Yoo, B. & Donthu, N. (1998), *Validating Hofstede's five-dimensional measure of culture at the individual level*. American Marketing Association, Summer Marketing Educators' *Conference*, Boston, USA

Online Images

Fig. 1: *Three levels of uniqueness in human mental programming*, Hofstede, G. (1997), *Cultures and Organizations: Software of the mind*, First Edition 1991, McGraw-Hill, New York, USA

Fig. 2: *What Germans mean when they say...*, viewed 20 February 2005, www.german-business-etiquette.com/13-what-germans-mean.html

Fig. 3: *Geert Hofstede*, viewed 27 July 2005, <http://geert-hofstede.international-business-center.com>

Fig. 4: *Edward T. Hall*, Center for Spatially integrated Social Science, viewed 13 July 2005, <www.csiss.org/classics/content/13>

Fig. 5: *40th Anniversary - Elysée Treaty*, viewed 20 February 2005, <www.auswaertiges-amt.de>

Fig. 6: *Voisins et enemies - La guerre des caricatures entre Paris et Berlin (1848-1890)*, viewed 28 July 2005, Ursula Koch; in: J.-C. Gardes et D. Poncin (ed.): L'étranger dans l'image satirique. Poitiers 1994, S. 73-96 <http://geogate.geographie.unimarburg.de/parser/parser.php?file=/deuframat/deutsch/3/3_2/mommsen/kap_3.htm>

Fig. 7: *Reconciliation between Adenauer and de Gaulle*, Süddeutsche Zeitung, 7 September 1962

Fig. 8: *The academic mobility between Germany and France*, Meyer-Kalkus, R., Bonn: DAAD-Forum 16, 1994; Statistisches Jahrbuch der Bundesrepublik Deutschland

Fig. 9: *Need a strong management. "This feels good!"*, taken from Breuer, P. & de Bartha, P. (2002), Deutsch-Französische Geschäftsbeziehungen erfolgreich managen, Fachverlag Deutscher Wirtschaftsdienst GmbH & CO. KG, Köln, Germany

Fig. 10: *Meeting between German and French*, Wirtschaftswoche, taken from Breuer, P. & de Bartha, P. (2002), Deutsch-Französische Geschäftsbeziehungen erfolgreich managen, Fachverlag Deutscher Wirtschaftsdienst GmbH & CO. KG, Köln, Germany

Appendix A: Questionnaire Interviewees

<u>GENERAL INFORMATION</u>

1. In which form are/were you involved with the French/Germans?

2. How long have you been in Germany/France?

3. Did you have any experiences abroad before your stay in France/Germany?

4. Did you have any fears before going abroad?

5. What did you think about the French/Germans before you arrived?

6. What was your first impression regarding life/people?

7. How did you come in contact with local people?

8. Have you been invited to people's homes?

INTERCULTURAL PROBLEMS / DIFFICULTIES AT WORK AND IN PRIVATE LIFE

1. Did you notice any significant differences between the German and the French culture?

   _____

2. Which of these difficulties do you look upon favourably?

   _____
   _____

3. What intercultural misunderstandings have you recognized by collaborating with Germans / French colleagues (e.g. behaviour, dealing with criticism, boss-employee relationship, greeting, physical contact ..)? Please describe a specific situation – if possible.

   _____
   _____

4. Was the outcome of the misunderstanding discussed among the participants?

   _____
   _____

5. Were you able to overcome these difficulties?

   ☐ Yes   ☐ no   ☐ partly

   If yes, how?

   _____
   _____

6. What intercultural misunderstandings have you recognized in social life?

   _____
   _____

7. What are, in your opinion, the most important reasons for these misunderstandings?

   _____
   _____

8. In what way did the experience with the other culture change your behaviour?

   _____
   _____

PREPARATION FOR THE COOPERATION WITH FRENCH/GERMAN COLLEAGUES

1. Did you receive adequate preparation for the collaboration with your French/German colleagues?

    ☐ yes   ☐ no

    If yes, how?

    ☐ seminar   ☐ company-initiated exchange of information with colleagues familiar with the other culture

    ☐ other: _____

2. Did you prepare yourself for collaborating with your French/German colleagues?

    ☐ yes   ☐ no

    If yes, in which way?

    ☐ seminar   ☐ talked with experienced friends

    ☐ literature   ☐ other: _____

3. Would you have preferred a better preparation by your company concerning your activities with French/Germans?

    ☐ yes   ☐ no   ☐ not necessary

4. What kind of preparation should this be / would produce the most effective results in your opinion?

    _____
    _____

PERSONAL INFORMATION:

- Name: _____
- Age: _____
- Employer: _____
- Position / Job Title: _____
- Nationality: _____

Declaration of authorship

Name of graduand: Sarah-Jane Pill

Name of supervisor: Prof. Dr. Waldmann

Bachelor's thesis topic: Understanding the Intercultural Differences Between Germans and French in the Working Environment. An Empirical Analysis through Application of the Cultural Assimilator.

1. I hereby declare that I am the true and sole author of the bachelor's thesis, that it has not been used in any previous examination procedures, that only mentioned sources and materials have been used and that all direct and indirect quotations have been marked as such according to § 31 Abs. 7 RaPO (Rahmenprüfungsordnung{ XE "Rahmenprüfungsordnung" } für die Fachhochschulen in Bayern)

Deggendorf, _____   _____
            Date   Graduand's signature

2. I hereby agree to my thesis being made available to the general public through the university library.

    no
    yes, after completion of the examination procedure
    yes, after a time of _____ years

I hereby declare that I am the sole copyright owner of the content bachelor's thesis, including all rights of disposal concerning all attached graphics, plans, etc. and no third party copyrights will be breached through publication.

Deggendorf, _____   _____
            Date   Graduand's signature

The supervisor is requested to fill out the following options if the author is in agreement with his/her thesis being made publicly accessible.

A copy of the bachelor's thesis should be added to the library inventory:

    I agree
    I disagree

Wissensquellen gewinnbringend nutzen

Qualität, Praxisrelevanz und Aktualität zeichnen unsere Studien aus. Wir bieten Ihnen im Auftrag unserer Autorinnen und Autoren Diplom-, Magister- und Staatsexamensarbeiten, Master- und Bachelorarbeiten, Dissertationen, Habilitationen und andere wissenschaftliche Studien und Forschungsarbeiten zum Kauf an. Die Studien wurden an Universitäten, Fachhochschulen, Akademien oder vergleichbaren Institutionen im In- und Ausland verfasst. Der Notendurchschnitt liegt bei 1,5.

Wettbewerbsvorteile verschaffen – Vergleichen Sie den Preis unserer Studien mit den Honoraren externer Berater. Um dieses Wissen selbst zusammenzutragen, müssten Sie viel Zeit und Geld aufbringen.

http://www.diplom.de bietet Ihnen unser vollständiges Lieferprogramm mit mehreren tausend Studien im Internet. Neben dem Online-Katalog und der Online-Suchmaschine für Ihre Recherche steht Ihnen auch eine Online-Bestellfunktion zur Verfügung. Eine inhaltliche Zusammenfassung und ein Inhaltsverzeichnis zu jeder Studie sind im Internet einsehbar.

Individueller Service – Für Fragen und Anregungen stehen wir Ihnen gerne zur Verfügung. Wir freuen uns auf eine gute Zusammenarbeit.

Ihr Team der Diplomarbeiten Agentur

Diplomica GmbH
Hermannstal 119k
22119 Hamburg

Fon: 040 / 655 99 20
Fax: 040 / 655 99 222

agentur@diplom.de
www.diplom.de

Printed in Germany
by Amazon Distribution
GmbH, Leipzig